Linking higher education and economic development

IMPLICATIONS FOR AFRICA FROM THREE SUCCESSFUL SYSTEMS

Pundy Pillay

HERANA   CHET

Published by the Centre for Higher Education Transformation (CHET),
House Vincent, First Floor, 10 Brodie Road, Wynberg Mews, Wynberg, 7800
Telephone: +27(0)21 763-7100 I Fax: +27(0)21 763-7117
E-mail: chet@chet.org.za I www.chet.org.za

© CHET 2010

ISBN 978-1-920355-44-9

Produced by COMPRESS.dsl I www.compressdsl.com

Cover illustration by Raymond Oberholzer

Distributed by African Minds
4 Eccleston Place, Somerset West, 7130, South Africa
info@africanminds.co.za
www.africanminds.co.za

For orders from outside Africa, excluding North America:
African Books Collective
orders@africanbookscollective.com
www.africanbookscollective.com

For orders from North America:
Michigan State University Press
msupress@msu.edu
http://msupress.msu.edu/

Contents

List of tables and boxes   v

List of acronyms and abbreviations   vi

Preamble   vii

Acknowledgements   ix

CHAPTER 1: **SYNTHESIS**

Introduction   1

Synthesis of the Finland case study   3

Synthesis of the South Korea case study   10

Synthesis of the North Carolina case study   16

The role of higher education in economic development   21

Common threads and differences   25

Some possible implications for African countries   26

CHAPTER 2: **FINLAND**

Education and the economy   33

The higher education system   35

Research and development   38

The regional role of higher education   41

Higher education and the innovation system   43

Higher education–industry linkages   45

Higher education and quality   48

Higher education–labour market linkages   50

Financing higher education   51

Recent changes in the Finnish system   52

Concluding observations and implications for African countries   53

CHAPTER 3: **NORTH CAROLINA**

The higher education system   55

The North Carolina Community College System   57

University–industry linkages: The case of NCSU   59

Identifying future challenges in higher education:
     The UNC Tomorrow Commission   63

Concluding observations and implications for African countries   68

CHAPTER 4: **SOUTH KOREA**

South Korean economic development   71

Education and economic development   73

Education financing   77

The higher education system   79

Higher education challenges   81

University–industry linkages   87

Concluding observations and implications for African countries   88

References   97
Appendix 1: List of interviewees   98
Appendix 2: Recommendations of the UNC Tomorrow Commission   100

List of tables and boxes

TABLES

Table 1:   Some socio-economic indicators – Finland, South Korea
            and the Unired States (2006–2008)   2

Table 2:   Higher education and economic development in Finland,
            South Korea and North Carolina – common threads
            and differences   25

Table 3:   State R&D expenditure by institution type, Finland   38

Table 4:   Comparative GDP per capita: South Korea, sub-Saharan Africa,
            OECD (USD)   71

Table 5:   Gross enrolment ratios by gender, South Korea (2005)   74

Table 6:   Ratio of private to national/public institutions,
            South Korea (2005)   78

Table 7:   Enrolment ratio of private to national/public institutions,
            South Korea (2005)   78

Table 8:   Number of institutions and students by type of institution,
            South Korea (2004)   81

Table 9:   Types of collaboration between industry and academia
            in South Korea   88

BOXES

Box 1:   Key implications for African countries   30

Box 2:   Nokia – a case study   47

Box 3:   The Finland experience: Possible implications for Africa   54

Box 4:   Major findings of the Tomorrow Commission   64

Box 5:   The North Carolina experience: Possible implications for Africa   69

Box 6:   Korea Research Institute for Vocational Education and Training
            (KRIVET)   82

Box 7:   Brain Korea 21   92

Box 8:   The South Korean experience: Possible implications for Africa   95

List of acronyms and abbreviations

BK21	Brain Korea 21
CESR	Center for Efficient, Secure and Reliable Computing
CHET	Centre for Higher Education Transformation
EUR	Euro
GDP	gross domestic product
GNP	gross national product
HEMA	Higher Education Masters in Africa
HERANA	Higher Education Research and Advocacy Network in Africa
ICT	information and communication technology
KAIST	Korea Advanced Institute of Science and Technology
KEDI	Korea Education Development Institute
KRIVET	Korea Research Institute for Vocational Education and Training
MoE	Ministry of Education
MoEE	Ministry of Employment and the Economy
NCCCS	North Carolina Community College System
NCRC	Non-woven Cooperative Research Center
NCSU	North Carolina State University
NURI	New University for Regional Innovation
OECD	Organisation for Economic Co-operation and Development
PISA	Programme for International Student Assessment
PRI	public research institution
POSTECH	Pohang University of Science and Technology
R&D	research and development
SBTDC	Small Business Technology Development Centre (North Carolina)
SCI	Science Citation Index
Tekes	National Funding Agency (Finland)
TIMSS	Trends in International Mathematics and Science Study
UNC	University of North Carolina
UNCGA	University of North Carolina General Administration
USD	US dollars
VTT	Technical Research Centre of Finland

Preamble

The Higher Education Research and Advocacy Network in Africa (HERANA) was established in 2007. The Network is co-ordinated by the Centre for Higher Education Transformation in Cape Town, South Africa. Key partners include the University of the Western Cape (South Africa), Makerere University (Uganda) and the University of Oslo (Norway). The research component of HERANA is investigating the complex relationships between higher education and development in the African context, with a specific focus on economic development and democracy. A second research area is exploring the use of research in policy-making. Alongside the research component is an advocacy strategy that aims to disseminate the findings of the research projects, better co-ordinate existing sources of information on higher education in Africa, develop a media strategy, and put in place a policy dialogue series (via seminars and information technology) that facilitates interactions between researchers, institutional leaders and decision-makers. The capacity building component of HERANA is the Higher Education Masters in Africa (HEMA) Programme which is run jointly between the key partners. The main objective of the HEMA Programme is to contribute to the strengthening of higher education in Africa through building capacity with respect to expertise on African higher education.

The research and advocacy components of HERANA are funded by the Carnegie Corporation of New York, the Ford Foundation, the Rockefeller Foundation and the Kresge Foundation. The HEMA programme is funded by NOMA (Nordic Masters in Africa).

The project on which this book is based forms part of a broader study on Universities and Economic Development in Africa, the aims of which include the following:

- At the national level, to explore the relationship between economic policy and development, on the one hand, and higher education system development, on the other; and
- At the institutional/project level, to understand the ways in which selected universities in Africa are responding to calls for a stronger engagement with the socio-economic development of their country and surrounding regions, with a specific emphasis on the role of the university in development, the strength of the academic core, and the institutionalisation of development projects.

The point of departure for the national component was to undertake a review of the international literature on the relationship between higher education and economic development, as well as in-depth case studies of three systems which have successfully linked their economic development and higher education policy and planning. The aim of these case studies would be to identify and distil the key characteristics of the ways in which higher education and economic development are linked in order to provide a framework for the collection and analysis of data in the eight African countries in the broader project (Botswana, Ghana, Kenya, Mauritius, Mozambique, South Africa, Tanzania and Uganda).

The three successful systems selected for inclusion in the study were Finland, South Korea and the state of North Carolina in the United States. The rationale for this selection is outlined in the introduction to Chapter 1. The research team visited the three systems between March and September 2008 and conducted interviews with individuals from a wide range of higher education institutions and government agencies. (See Appendix 1 for the full list of interviewees.) Additional information was gleaned from institutional documents and other reports.

This book presents the findings of this project. In Chapter 1, the key findings from the three case studies are synthesised. The detailed individual case studies of the three systems are presented in Chapters 2, 3 and 4.

Acknowledgements

This study would not have been possible without the support and participation of the following organisations and individuals:

Funding
The Carnegie Corporation of New York, the Ford Foundation, the Rockefeller Foundation and the Kresge Foundation.

Senior researchers
Dr Pundy Pillay and Dr Nico Cloete (Centre for Higher Education Transformation, South Africa).

Researchers
Dr James Nkata (Makerere University, Uganda) and Mr Romulo Pinheiro (University of Oslo, Norway).

Project manager
Tracy Bailey (Centre for Higher Education Transformation, South Africa).

Interview respondents
Finland
Professors Seppo Hölttä and Timo Aarrevaara (University of Tampere); Dr Paulla Nybergh (Head of Innovation Division, Ministry of Employment and the Economy); Dr Rita Asplund (Research Director, The Research Institute of the Finnish Economy); Dr Antii Moisio, Ms Tanja Kirjavainen and Dr Roope Uusitalo (Government Institute for Economic Research); Mr Ossi Tuomi (Director of Development, University of Helsinki and former Secretary General, Finnish Higher Education Evaluation Council); Dr Esko-Olavi Sepphala (Secretary General, Ministry of Education, Science and Technology Policy Council); and, Professor Wim Naude (Senior Research Fellow, World Institute for Development Economics Research).

North Carolina
Dr Alan Mabe (Vice-President, Academic Planning and University-School Programmes, University of North Carolina System); Ms Willa Dickens (Vice-President, Economic Workforce Development, North Carolina Community College System); Dr James Zuiches (Vice-Chancellor, Office of Extension, Engagement and Economic Development, North Carolina State University); Professor Helen Ladd (Professor of Social Policy, Terry Sanford Public Policy Institute, Duke University); Professor Carol Kasworm (Head, Department of Adult and Higher Education, North Carolina State University); Professor Charles Clotfelter (Professor of Public Policy, Terry Sanford Institute, Duke University).

South Korea
Dr Kang Byung-Woon (Director, Research Institute for Higher Education), Dr Dong Kwang Kim (Director, Department of External Relations) and Ms Sarah Han (Researcher,

Department of External Relations) at the Korean Council for University Education; Professor Se-Jung Oh (Dean, College of Natural Sciences), Professor Young Kuk (Vice-President, Research Affairs / Head, Industry-Academic Cooperation Foundation / Chief Executive Officer, SNU Industry Foundation), Professor Keouk (Korbil) Kim (Department of Education and Graduate Students) and Professor Suk Ho Chung (Director, School of Mechanical Engineering and Aerospace Engineering) at the Seoul National University; Dr Ji-Seong Ryu (Senior Research Fellow, Human Resources Management Department), Ms Wuran Kang (Chief Researcher, HRM Department) and Dr Hyungmin Jung (Research Fellow, Macroeconomics) at the Samsung Economic Research Institute; Professor Ju Ho Lee (Education and Labour Market Economist, KDI-School); Dr Mi-Sug Jin (Director, Department of Human Resources Research, Korea Research Institute for Vocational Education and Training); and, Dr Jung Yoon Choi (Korea Education Development Institute).

Critical readers
Professor David Dill and Dr Jim Sadler (University of North Carolina at Chapel Hill, United States), Dr Misug Jin (Korea Research Institute for Vocational Education and Training, South Korea) and Prof Timo Aarrevaara (University of Helsinki, Finland).

Editing and proofreading
Nico Cloete, Tracy Bailey and Michelle Willmers.

CHAPTER 1
Synthesis

Introduction

This is a synthesis of the findings from three international case studies on the relationship between higher education and economic development. The three case studies are Finland, South Korea, and the state of North Carolina in the United States.

This sample of country case studies was chosen for several reasons. First, all of them reflect, to a greater or lesser degree, examples of well developed higher education systems comprising different types of institutions with varying impacts on development. Second, the higher education system in Finland and South Korea, but to a lesser extent in North Carolina, is characterised by high levels of participation – in fact, the highest in the world. Third, there is, in all three cases in higher education, evidence of a strong and close relationship between education and economic development in general, and higher education and economic development in particular. In all three systems a rethink of the major economic policies were accompanied by a deliberate attempt to link higher education to economic development.

Notwithstanding the fact that all three systems are located in the developed country Organisation for Economic Co-operation and Development (OECD) industrialised context, the purpose of this research has been to flesh out the common themes around higher education and economic development, and to distil possible implications for African policy-makers.

Table 1 provides some socio-economic indicators for Finland, South Korea and the United States. In this table, socio-economic data are shown for the United States rather than for North Carolina because of the absence of comparable data for the latter. However, the United States figures may be an appropriate proxy for the state of North Carolina. North Carolina could at best be regarded as an 'average' state, and at worst just slightly below average.

> The purpose of this research has been to flesh out the common themes around higher education and economic development, and to distil possible implications for African policy-makers

Table 1

Some socio-economic indicators – Finland, South Korea and the United States (2006–2008)

Indicator	Finland	South Korea	United States
Population (m)	5	49	302
GDP per capita (USD)	44 400	19 690	46 040
Human Development Index			
Ranking (out of 179 countries)	11/174	26/174	12/174
Index	0.952	0.921	0.951
Expenditure on education (% of GDP)	6.4	4.2	5.6
Participation rates (gross enrolment ratio)	88	85	83
Combined GER for primary, secondary, tertiary	101	96	93
Tertiary education expenditure as % of education budget	33	13	Not available
Institutional typology	Universities, polytechnics – almost entirely public	Universities, junior and senior vocational colleges – public and (mainly) private	Universities, community colleges, other colleges – public and private

GDP = gross domestic product; GER = gross enrolment ratio
Sources: World Bank (2008); UNDP (2008)

A common thread that runs through all three case studies is the acceptance, at the present time, of the knowledge economy. In all three cases there has been a close link historically between developments in education and in the economy. In the case of Finland and South Korea, education planning, specifically higher education, has been closely linked to changes in the pattern of economic development, initially from the production of primary commodities, through dominance by the manufacturing sector, to the services sector and particularly today, the knowledge-based economy. In North Carolina, on the other hand, little formal state planning takes place either for economic or educational development. Nevertheless, the close linkages between the state education system, the private sector and higher education institutions have enabled the state to address the higher education challenges of industrial transformation towards the knowledge economy.

> A common thread that runs through all three case studies is the acceptance of the knowledge economy

The next three sections describe the higher education systems and findings from the analysis of the case studies respectively in Finland, South Korea and North Carolina. The concluding section, has three parts: (a) findings relating specifically to the relationship between higher education and economic development; (b) a summary of the common features and differences in the three regions; and (c) possible implications for African countries.

Synthesis of the Finland case study

Introduction
Finland was chosen as a case study for this project for several reasons. First, it has a well-known reputation for having one of the best education systems in the world in terms of access and quality. Second, there is a very high participation rate in higher education. Third, there is substantial evidence of a close link between education and economic development. Fourth, the development of the higher education system has occurred in a political milieu in which equity in all its dimensions is regarded as being of paramount importance.

A feature of the education and economic systems in Finland is also the predominant role of the state, particularly with regard to education financing, planning in both sectors, and creating an environment in which all sectors (public, private and higher education institutions) can flourish in addressing the needs of the knowledge economy.

There are several features of the Finnish political economy that are crucial to an understanding of the relationship between higher education and economic development. Foremost amongst these factors is a long-standing and unshakeable commitment to equity in all its forms (gender, region, socio-economic status). Second, as a strong proponent of the Nordic welfare state model, the role of the Finnish government in higher education is all-embracing and reflected, inter alia, in the high levels of resourcing for the sector and in the commitment to both the education and research roles of higher education. Third, there is a strong commitment to consensus-building in general on the part of all the social partners (government, private business and civil society).

Education and the economy
Finland's economy was dramatically diversified during the past two decades, especially in the period following the collapse of the Soviet Union, an event that triggered a severe economic crisis as a consequence of the close economic relationship between the two countries. In the face of this economic crisis, the government took two important policy decisions: first, to further develop the Nordic welfare model; and second, to invest substantially in the development of the knowledge economy. In line with this economic policy decision, the role of higher education assumed much greater importance in the 1990s.

The state's investment in education generally, and in higher education in particular, is relatively high in both international and OECD terms. In addition, the state invests substantially in research and development (R&D) spending.

Finland's national objective is 'sustainable and balanced social and economic development'. High employment, productivity and competitiveness are key factors. A high-quality higher education system as well as measures to increase research and technological development play a significant part in attempts to attain the country's national development goals.

The higher education system

The main characteristics of the higher education system include the following: a comprehensive, dual-sector comprising 20 universities and 29 polytechnics spread over the whole country; a high participation rate; and the public nature of the system including extensive state funding.

The dual structure has several special characteristics:

- The two higher education sub-sectors are fundamentally different. The polytechnics are seen as institutions which prepare their students for practical work, while the mission of universities is more academic and has a theoretical and research orientation.
- The degrees and degree programmes are different in polytechnics and universities. The universities have a two-cycle degree structure (Bachelor-Master) while the polytechnics have so far had only one level of degrees (Bachelor). A three-year pilot of postgraduate polytechnic degrees was launched in 2002.
- The model of administration is different in the universities and the polytechnics. The universities are maintained by the state, while the polytechnics are run by municipalities, joint municipal bodies and foundations.
- The administrative structure and staff categories of universities are largely geared to support research, while polytechnics are mainly institutes of teaching, with fewer research-related tenures.
- The funding systems are geared to support the special mission of each sector. In universities, external funding is largely targeted toward research. At first, polytechnics obtained funds for the development of their basic operations and later for teaching and the regional service functions.

Research and development

There are three prominent features in the R&D landscape:

- High levels of public and private spending
- Appropriate institutional arrangements for the distribution of resources, and for strategic policy development and coordination, and
- An overwhelming sense of collaboration between and consensus amongst the various stakeholders, including government, higher education institutions, public research institutes, public funding agencies, and the private business sector.

There is a strong emphasis on R&D and the universities, as well as the polytechnics to a lesser extent, have an important role in the R&D function.

In 2003, R&D expenditure was EUR5 billion, equivalent to 3.5% of GDP. Higher education sector expenditure (universities, polytechnics and university central hospitals) in this regard was EUR976 million, or about 19% of overall expenditure. The business sector accounted for 70% and the public sector (mainly state research institutes) 10%. At 1% of GDP, public R&D funding is amongst the highest in the world (the European Union's average is 0.77%).

State R&D funding flows largely to the Ministry of Education (MoE) and the Ministry of Employment and the Economy (MoEE) after consensus on national priorities and direction has been reached in the Science and Technology Policy Council, which is chaired by the Prime Minister. Higher education institutions receive core research funding but may also access funds from the Academy of Finland (MoE) on a competitive basis for basic research, and from the National Funding Agency (Tekes) (MoEE) for technological research.

The regional role of higher education
An important feature of Finnish development is the commitment to equitable regional development policies to ensure balanced national development. Higher education was appropriately decentralised in line with the evolving politically decentralised framework comprising regional councils.

The higher education system of 20 universities and 29 polytechnics covers the whole country. Higher education has been developed as a dual system, in which each sector has a profile of its own. The universities are charged with academic research and education based on it and the polytechnics with higher education geared to the world of work, and R&D which serves education, the world of work and regional development.

> An important feature of Finnish development is the commitment to equitable regional development policies to ensure balanced national development

The university system grew into the present regionally comprehensive network during the 1960s and 1970s. The present 20 universities are based in 11 cities and towns, providing degree education in over 20 different localities. The aim of the regionally decentralised network is to make full use of the talent of the entire country and to produce a highly educated workforce for the needs of the growing public and business sectors.

In the 1980s, universities were increasingly seen as engines of regional development. This trend gained impetus from the improved possibilities for universities and the private sector to develop research cooperation. In the 1990s, the focus in university development was on quality. At that time the polytechnic system was also being created.

Polytechnic education is currently being developed in two dimensions: as a network of degree education and as a service network providing extension education (e.g. adult education) and other services. The aim is to build a network in which all the degree education units are large enough to provide high quality education and to conduct high quality R&D in support of their regions. The structure and provision of polytechnics will be developed to enable them to become key factors in their regions, supporting local municipalities, businesses and work communities, and catering for local residents' self-development aspirations.

The activities of the decentralised higher education network are underpinned by the universities' and polytechnics' mutually complementary knowledge production, which in turn is based on their respective strengths. Collaboration and structural development promote the emergence of sufficiently large and diverse units needed to ensure the quality of education and research.

Higher education and the innovation system

The higher education system forms the basis for a regionally comprehensive innovation system. The system is being developed as an entity which is both internationally competitive and responsive to regional needs.

At present universities and polytechnics are seen to be key components in the national and regional innovation systems, in which they operate in close interaction with business and industry, and other regional players. As a result of the current technological advances and knowledge-intensive operations, economic and social development is increasingly built on human capital. This means that the higher education institutions have a growing role in producing new knowledge and diffusing knowledge and know-how in an increasingly globalised and knowledge-based economy.

The challenge for Finnish higher education institutions is to strike a balance between being internationally competitive in terms of teaching and research, and being sensitive to the education and research needs of their local regions.

In the division of labour between universities and polytechnics in research, universities are responsible for scientific research and education based on it, including researcher training. Doctorates are awarded only by universities. Polytechnics mainly conduct R&D which caters for working-life needs, serves teaching, supports industrial life and regional development, and is based on the industrial structure of the region. Universities also maintain most of the scientific and research infrastructure, which is funded through the university budget.

> Universities are responsible for scientific research and education. Polytechnics conduct R&D which caters for working-life needs, serves teaching, supports industrial life and regional development, and is based on the industrial structure of the region

Key success factors in the development of the innovation system include the following:

- The high quality of education at all levels
- Economic factors, especially high economic growth and the commitment to a knowledge economy
- High commitment to public and private financing of R&D
- Excellent cooperation between public and private sectors, between government departments, between higher education institutions, and between higher education institutions and the private sector
- Incentives provided by Tekes, the national funding agency (e.g. providing matching grants to the private sector and insisting that university research must be relevant)

- Political consensus and citizens' support for R&D, and
- Mutual trust between science, technology and innovation players.

Higher education–industry linkages

Tekes funding has played a prominent role in promoting co-operation between higher education institutions and the private sector. Tekes aims to enhance the competitiveness of manufacturing and service industries by financing and activating product development and R&D projects conducted by companies and by universities, polytechnics and research institutes. Tekes has financed the development of the technological knowledge base of universities and polytechnics and their cooperation with business and industry.

The 'Centres of Expertise' programme administered by the Ministry of Interior encourages the regions to utilise their top expertise in order to strengthen the competitiveness of the region. There are 22 centres of expertise. The programme seeks to enhance the innovation environments in regions by improving cooperation between the research sector and local business and industry. The centres of expertise are mostly run by the local science/technology park. Technology/science parks also implement the TULI (from research to business) programme financed by Tekes, which seeks to identify research-business ideas – especially in universities, polytechnics and research institutes – and offers expert services to research teams and researchers in commercialising ideas.

Universities and polytechnics offer several different support services relating to research and innovation. The most important services relate to the acquisition of R&D funding and contractual procedures. In addition, they offer careers and recruitment services to students and employers while some higher education institutions offer incubator services to students. Universities and polytechnics also offer different extension as well as piloting and testing services to business.

The Nokia experience, for example, shows how mutually beneficial the R&D experience has been to a range of actors including Nokia itself, other private sector companies and higher education institutions.

Higher education-labour market linkages

In many respects the higher education system has met the labour market challenges with a high degree of success, especially in comparison with other OECD countries.

A distinguishing feature is the central role assigned to labour market demand in the allocation of resources for higher education. State-funded study places are the central resource allocated by most Ministries of Education, and in Finland these are primarily allocated according to forecasts of labour market needs. These forecasts of labour market needs, adjusted to reflect policy targets for the government, then become the basis for a national Development Plan, a document that provides a five-year framework for education

> Finland has a system of enrolment resource allocation that is not driven by student demand, but according to forecasts of labour market demand

Synthesis

supply. The Development Plan provides the framework within which negotiations between the MoE and individual higher education institutions take place. Intake for each field of education is agreed between them, and contained in each institution's performance agreement with the Ministry. Seen in this light, Finland has a system of enrolment resource allocation that is not driven by student demand, but according to forecasts of labour market demand.

Higher education graduates fare significantly better in labour markets than do those without tertiary qualifications. If one compares all higher education graduates to those with secondary qualifications, rates of unemployment are lower and wages higher. Polytechnic graduates occupy a middle position between secondary schooling and university graduates, both with respect to rates of unemployment and wages. And, among university graduates, the rate of unemployment diminishes, and wages increase as the level of qualification increases.

In many respects the system of higher education has connections to working life that are an international benchmark against which other systems might be judged. Those who complete a tertiary degree have high rates of employment, a significant wage premium, and private returns that compare favourably to those of graduates in other nations. This suggests that the relationship between the demand and supply of graduates is, on balance, holding up well.

Higher education and equity

The main goal of public policy has been to provide equal opportunities for students from different backgrounds (i.e. irrespective of socio-economic status, gender, place of residence). In the case of Finnish higher education, the government has sought to level out the field first and foremost by means of comprehensive basic education, but just as importantly by increasing study places in higher education with a view to equal opportunity in regional terms.

Probably the most important measure taken to promote equal opportunity has been the regional expansion of the university sector. With regional policy, efforts have been made to guarantee equal opportunity for young people to participate in university education, irrespective of their place of residence.

Probably the most important measure taken to promote equal opportunity has been the regional expansion of the university sector

Equity has been an important factor in post-war educational reform. The accessibility of higher education has increased remarkably, mainly through gradual improvement of comprehensive basic education, wide geographical distribution of university education, and strong expansion of the polytechnic sector. One of the main arguments behind the expansion has been to include new groups in higher education and to reduce inequalities in gender, place of residence and social class.

Financing higher education

The role of the state in funding higher education is overwhelming. The following data reveal the extent of the state's role in this regard:

- In 2002 public expenditure on higher education, both on institutions and subsidies to households, comprised 2.1% of GDP, the fourth highest amongst 28 OECD countries for which data are available. Public expenditure on higher education grew 18% in real terms between 1999–2000 and 2004–2005, most of which was due to an expansion of enrolments (13%) and a modest share due to increased expenditures per student (4%).
- Finland is distinctive in its reliance on public financing for tertiary education. In 2002 more than 96% of all expenditures on higher education institutions were from public sources.

New changes in the Finnish system

A new University Act, effective from January 2010, brings about important changes to the way in which institutions are governed. In terms of the new Act, universities are required to appoint 40% of their board members from outside the institution. Three further reforms were proposed in the new legislation. First, there will be a major change to the way rectors are appointed. Like most of Europe, Finnish rectors have been elected by the professors, other staff and students. In future, the board will appoint the rector who will be answerable to that board. The appointee will not need to be a professor of the university, as is currently required.

Second, universities' legal status will change: they will become independent legal entities rather than continuing to be 'accounting units' within the government bureaucracy. University staff will cease to be 'civil servants' and some have seen this change as an attack on academic freedom.

Finally, universities will have two-thirds ownership of companies that own university buildings and the government will be the minority shareholder. At present, universities rent buildings from a government-owned company, so the new legislation should provide universities with an asset they can use as leverage for borrowing from the capital markets.

There are important implications of the new legislation. First, it increases the role that outside stakeholders can play in the university. Second, it also increases university autonomy, particularly through giving them more responsibility for financing and staff policies. It is hoped that the reforms will create an environment in which universities can start to expand their funding base by acquiring funds from other sources, although this seems unlikely in the short term. Moreover, there is no intention at this stage to introduce tuition fees for domestic students.

Synthesis of the South Korea case study

Introduction

There are several reasons for the choice of South Korea as a case study. First, amongst recently-industrialised countries, its education system shows rapid expansion at all levels in a relatively short period. Second, the schooling system has achieved a very high level of quality as reflected in the country's performance in international tests in mathematics and science. Third, there is a very high participation rate in higher education, second only to Finland's worldwide. Fourth, there is a very close functional linkage between changes in economic development patterns and policies, and education policies.

There are similarities and differences with Finland with respect to the role of the state. Like Finland, the state plays a dominant role in the funding of school (mainly primary) education. Also, like Finland, the state plays a key planning role in the economy, and in ensuring that the education system develops in line with the human resource needs of the former. However, unlike Finland, the state plays a relatively minor role in the funding of higher education – the Korean system is predominantly private.

> The rapid expansion of education at all levels is the outstanding feature of South Korean educational development during the country's industrialisation

Education and the economy

Education has been a key factor in South Korea's rapid economic growth over the past four decades. Since the 1960s, the government-led economic development plans have been directly reflected in education policy and planning. The government has been generally successful in providing and expanding the education system based on the human resource needs of the economy. As a result, the education system has developed in tandem with the various stages of economic development. The focus of the government's educational planning moved from primary to secondary education and finally to the tertiary level, according to the nation's economic advancement. The rapid expansion of education at all levels is the outstanding feature of Korean educational development during the country's industrialisation.

The education system has been successful at the primary and secondary levels in providing equal educational access, irrespective of gender, geographical location and socio-economic background. The rate of pupil retention is nearly 100% in the lower grades. Moreover, South Korea's education system at the school level has achieved quality improvements in tandem with quantitative expansion, as reflected in the country's performances in international tests in mathematics and science. Quality improvements have also been due to efforts outside the formal schooling system in a well developed private tutoring system which functions as an established industry across the country. Thus the costs of schooling are quite high when these private costs are added and efficiency (a comparison of inputs and outputs) much lower than official figures indicate.

The higher education system

South Korea's rate of educational expansion at the tertiary level has been remarkable. During the 1970s and 1980s, higher education was expanded in two ways: increased student enrolment, and diversified institutions of higher education. As 'junior' colleges (providing two-year vocational programmes) took a larger share of tertiary education, their programmes were diversified to meet industrial needs. Higher education continued to expand during the 1990s. The main areas of expansion were two-year colleges and fields of engineering and natural sciences at four-year colleges and universities.

In general, the government's expansion policy for higher education has been effective in terms of supplying highly qualified, white-collar workers and R&D personnel according to each stage of economic development. Specifically, the government's control over the enrolment quotas during the 1960s and 1970s played a key role in balancing the demand and supply of college graduates in the labour market, consequently reducing inefficiency in the national economy and social problems that resulted from the oversupply and underemployment of college graduates. However, in the 21st century, the demands of an increasingly globalised and knowledge-based economy have exposed the shortfalls in the quality of the outputs from the higher education system, and the ability of graduates to cope with the demands of the labour market.

As a result of expansion that has occurred over the last 20 years, South Korea now has the highest rate of participation in higher education of any country in the world, with the possible exception of Finland. This remarkable expansion was possible because of the high quality of and high completion rates in secondary education. The completion rate of secondary school increased from 46% in 1970 to almost 100% by 1999. South Korea has thereby become one of the first countries to have nearly universal completion of secondary education. Currently, more than 80% of all secondary school graduates go on to tertiary education.

In 1945, when South Korea was liberated from Japanese rule, there was only one national university. Seven national universities were established during the period 1951–1953; making the modern system of universities in South Korea little more than 50 years old.

The period between 1960 and 1980 was largely concerned with economic development and the links of education to economic growth, marked by an emphasis on science and the establishment of vocational schools (now junior colleges). The real expansion of universities and colleges took place initially during the 1960s, but also during the 1980s when there was a 30% increase in student numbers, and during the 1990s. Legislation passed in 1995 facilitated the establishment of new universities and two-year colleges. Between 1990 and 2004, the number of tertiary institutions increased from 265 to 419; the number of students from 1.7 million to 3.5 million; the number of academic staff from 43 000 to 67 000; and the number of administrative staff from under 33 000 to more than 38 000.

Universities of many kinds dominate tertiary education. These provide four-year programmes leading to a baccalaureate degree. The majority of universities are nominally private with government-sponsored (national or public) universities enrolling only 22% of university students.

Most universities are comprehensive, providing teaching in a broad range of sciences, social sciences, the humanities and professional subjects like engineering and business. However, some are limited to technical subjects.

The second dominant type of institution is the college, which now enrols about 40% of students in tertiary education. Most programmes last two years, though about 10% of students are enrolled in three-year programmes, especially in the sciences, engineering and other technical fields. These institutions exist to prepare middle-level human resources and technicians; the fields of study include a range of occupations in engineering, health including nursing, business and law, and education.

South Korean colleges now enrol about 40% of students in tertiary education

Compared to universities, a much larger proportion of colleges and college enrolments are in the private sector. This in turn means that colleges are more reliant on tuition fees and less on government funding; they also do not receive government funding for research, as some universities do. On the other hand, colleges appear to be more closely related to employers than universities are; it is more common for colleges to set up partnerships with local firms, and they often offer customised training, in which firms pay for short-term training adapted to their purposes.

Research and innovation

A distinctive feature of research and development in South Korea is the strong part played by private companies. In the context of a national concern to improve the contribution of research and development to economic performance, this raises key questions about the role that tertiary education should play in national research policies.

In terms of the volume of overall R&D, Korean universities play a relatively small role. About 76% of overall spending on R&D is carried out by corporations; 14% is carried out by research institutes; and only 10% is done in universities – a proportion that has increased only slightly over the past decade, from about 7% in 1993. Given the prominent role of Korean firms in R&D, it is unlikely that universities will become major players in the foreseeable future – particularly since a great deal of current R&D funded by firms is intended to develop new products, a kind of firm-specific and market-driven form of R&D that is less appropriate for universities.

Overall then, the role of universities in national R&D is quite small at present although there are indications that this has been changing somewhat (especially in the case of Seoul National University) since 2002. There are, however, two roles in which universities are particularly important. One is the support of basic research, as distinct from commercial research. While universities carried out only 10% of overall R&D, university faculty contributed 76% of the scientific papers written in South Korea. The second role relates to the training of potential researchers in which universities naturally have a predominant role.

As stated earlier, most applied research has been left to the government research institutes and private sector. The institutions of higher education in general were not really interested in or willing to build up competencies in engineering and science. To strengthen the research capacity of universities, the Ministry of Education set up a plan suggesting two large projects: the second phase of 'Brain Korea 21' (BK21), and the Five-Year Plan for the Development of Basic Sciences. South Korea's aim for the two projects is to have about 15 universities with world-class reputations by 2010. The second BK21 will be more focused on science and technology, while the Five-Year Plan is for the humanities and social sciences. The former project is being planned in close cooperation with the ministries dealing with hi-tech or national strategic industries.

> Two roles in which universities are particularly important:
> - the support of basic research, as distinct from commercial research
> - the training of potential researchers

A very important feature of BK21 is that it rates and supports departments or research units, not individual academics, since it believes that research progress is made in teams. An important aspect of rating the team is that it must have international participation and it gets marks for relevance and disadvantage.

BK21 has come under strong criticism for favouring a small number of large-scale, research-orientated universities in general, but it is evident that BK21 has greatly improved the research capacity of universities. There is also some evidence that the amount of research funds that went into BK21 project teams had a positive impact on research productivity measured by research papers per faculty member. It is also known that the number of research papers written by the faculty members involved in BK21, which were published in the Science Citation Index journals, increased substantially between 1998 and 2003.

Higher education and regional development

Higher education provision in South Korea is skewed towards the big cities, particularly Seoul. To address inequities in regional provision, the government has started a new initiative. The New University for Regional Innovation (NURI) is a government-funded project for local universities that is aimed at diversification and specialisation, higher employment rates for local university graduates, and creating a greater role for local universities as centres of regional innovation by strengthening ties within a region, with local government, companies and research institutions.

The government is investing USD1.2 million in the NURI project, and the fund will be allocated to 13 cities and provinces based on population, number of students and universities. The project, which started in 2004, has not yet been assessed for its achievements. The Ministry of Education planned to conduct annual assessments and an interim assessment (in the third year of the project) which would include an assessment of budget execution and performance versus targets.

Higher education–industry linkages

Historically, as stated earlier, there has been poor interaction between universities and business with respect to research and innovation. One reason is that most large firms have built up their own training and education facilities. However, given the increasing demands of a knowledge-based economy, the need for a national innovation system based on greater cooperation between government research agencies, universities and the private sector appears to be paramount.

A number of initiatives have been started to facilitate this process. In an effort to foster proactive collaboration and create a channel for communicating the demands and needs of industry to the education community, the government is formulating a new industry-academia collaboration system, which is based on the 'Act on the Promotion of Industrial Education and Industry–Academia Collaboration'. Taking into consideration the diverse regional characteristics and unique circumstances of universities and industries, the Ministry of Education has classified cases of industry-academia collaboration into three groups. Policy implementation and financial support will eventually be closely tied to the collaborative system to create a university system that fully incorporates the industry–academia collaboration framework.

In addition to financial support, the government introduced two new features into the higher education system. One is a contract-based education system that enables close ties between industry and academia. This system has been established to allow the needs of the industrial sector to be directly reflected in the operation of the university curriculum. For example, new majors as well as departments can be established under contract between universities and private enterprises. The contract can stipulate matters related to the student quota, student selection process, curriculum, teaching and learning processes, and so forth. Upon graduation, students enrolled in the programme will receive favourable employment opportunities from the companies. The other feature is a school-enterprise system that enables the practical application of the research conducted through industry-academia collaboration.

The link between universities and industry is expected to get stronger because a new regional governance system, the Regional Innovation Committee (consisting of key stakeholders in each major city and province), has been established to facilitate communication among the key stakeholders. Financial support from both central and local governments is available; however, the collaboration among them is not as active as expected.

> The link between universities and industry is expected to get stronger because of a new regional governance system, the Regional Innovation Committee

Synthesis

Higher education and equity

Unlike in schooling, when it comes to equity in Korean higher education there are serious concerns with regard to gender, class and region. Gender differences in tertiary participation are relatively marked, and are linked to the overall role of women in Korean society and the labour market.

In order to enhance equity, South Korea has a number of grants, loans and other outreach programmes, intended to enhance the access of low-income students and women to private universities. In addition, the Ministry of Education uses its control over the admissions process to try to influence equity. Whether this approach is successful is unclear.

Higher education financing

Over the years, the growth rate of the education budget has outpaced that of GDP, as the government has put a high priority on education. From 1963 to 2005, the government's spending on education increased more than 29 times in real terms, while the GDP and the government's overall budget increased 20 times. The share of education in the total government budget had remained around 15% in the 1960s, but has increased since that time and reached more than 20% in the 2000s.

For secondary and higher education, a substantial amount of funding comes from the private sector, such as households and private foundations. At the secondary level, the private share is more than 40%, and at the tertiary level it is over 70%. Private financing accounts for about two-thirds of the total direct costs in education.

The heavy reliance on private funding in secondary and higher education has an important policy implication. Inducing the private sector to play a more active role in providing educational services at the secondary and higher educational levels would offer a leverage effect, allowing limited government resources to be spent on prioritised areas. Until recent years, by leaving higher levels of education to the private sector and targeting public resources for primary education, South Korea has been able to address one of the main equity issues: basic education for all.

While there is little doubt that higher private involvement in tertiary education has enabled the release of public resources for the universalisation of high quality basic education, at the same time it has reduced the leverage of the state to influence the outcomes of higher education in line with the needs of further economic and social development.

Only 0.5% of GDP is spent by government on higher education, as opposed to the 1% OECD average. The fact that the higher education system is dominated by private financing has important implications for economic development because it is evident in South Korea that the private component of the higher education system is not producing sufficient numbers of high quality graduates for the increasingly sophisticated economy.

Synthesis of the North Carolina case study

Introduction

The state of North Carolina was selected as a case study for a number of reasons. First, it is one of the fastest growing regions in the United States, attracting, in particular, a large number of professionals. Second, during the past few decades it has succeeded in changing the basis of the state's economy from one based on primary (e.g. tobacco) and secondary (e.g. textile manufacturing) activities to one dominated by tertiary-sector activities demanding inputs of highly educated labour. Third, the higher education system has developed in tandem with changes in the economy, and the region provides an excellent model of the respective roles of the state and the private sector in the higher education system and the economy. Fourth, North Carolina is also the site of one of the major research/technological parks in the United States, namely the Research Triangle. This site has attracted the research arms of many of the country's largest corporations. As a consequence, the Research Triangle is able to attract professional staff from all parts of the country. In addition, there is a close working relationship between institutions located in the park and the three high quality universities located in close proximity, namely, University of North Carolina (UNC), North Carolina State University (NCSU), and Duke University.

The higher education system

The higher education system has developed in tandem with changes in the economy, and the region provides an excellent model of the respective roles of the state and the private sector in higher education and the economy.

The higher education system comprises public universities, publicly-funded community colleges, a private university (Duke) and a number of private colleges. The 16 public universities constitute the UNC system. The private college sector receives state support for enrolled in-state students.

There are at least two areas where the state plays a particularly prominent role, namely with respect to funding and to engagement with institutions on the relationship between higher education and economic development. The state provides substantial funding to universities in the form of both line budget items for teaching and research, and conditional grants for specific projects. At NCSU, for example, state funding comprises between 30% and 47% of the university's revenue. State funding is provided for, inter alia, instruction, agricultural extension, research activities and special infrastructure projects. There is strong, general and specific support for higher education on the part of the state government and legislature, and a powerful sense of its importance for economic and social development.

There is a high level of productive engagement between higher education institutions and the private sector to deal with changing economic conditions. There are good linkages between universities and other post-secondary institutions (community colleges), linking higher education and economic development particularly with respect to a clear division of roles, as well as articulation.

There is some university specialisation in the public system. For example, in the Research Triangle area, the two major public institutions, UNC at Chapel Hill and UNC State University, rarely duplicate the high-cost faculties, such as medicine and engineering. However, there is little structural differentiation within the university system and growing evidence that all universities are aspiring to be 'world-class' teaching and research institutions.

The state university system is of varying quality but the large institutions are of very high quality. In a recent survey, UNC (Chapel Hill) was placed first among 120 national universities and colleges in terms of 'value for money' in public higher education institutions with respect to quality and cost, with NCSU placed thirteenth. Duke University, the only private university, is regarded as one of the best institutions in the country.

The public university system is much more unified than the system in many other American states, with all 16 institutions falling under one University of North Carolina General Administration (UNCGA). The president of the UNCGA is often a politically astute person with private sector experience and a serious commitment to higher education. For example, the 2007/2008 president was once a successful banker and also served as chief of staff in the Clinton White House.

There are two components to the North Carolina Community College System (NCCCS), namely continuing education (workforce development), and an associate degree, with graduates emerging with a two-year community college degree. The NCCCS is North Carolina's primary agency for the delivery of job training, literacy and adult education. The system served more than 800 000 students through its 58 institutions in the 2005/2006 academic year. The NCCCS is located in 90 counties across the state with 156 additional campuses or off-campus centres, in addition to the 58 main campuses with service areas of one or more counties.

The NCCCS is interesting, from a developing country perspective, for a number of reasons:

- It offers unlimited opportunities for students who are unable to go to university to pursue post-secondary education through the attainment of associate degrees.
- Those who qualify from a community college with an associate degree can then go on to university.
- Continuing education through workforce development and other adult education programmes is possible throughout one's life.
- The workforce development programmes to enhance skills provide a number of choices and are tuned to the wide-ranging needs of a growing economy.
- The success of the community college system is due in no small measure to the strong and productive relationships that have developed with universities, the private sector and government with respect both to funding and identifying educational and training opportunities to enhance economic development.

Indeed, the sense of partnership (between community colleges and the state, between community colleges and regional universities, and between community colleges and the state government) is overwhelming and undoubtedly an important factor in the success of the NCCCS.

University-industry linkages: The NCSU case

The NCSU provides an excellent case study of a higher education institution that has developed close, productive linkages with the private sector to promote economic development. NCSU has also demonstrated considerable creativity and entrepreneurship in its 552 United States patents and 533 active license agreements with industry to commercialise academic research. In the past 25 years, NCSU, operating as a knowledge base for the state, has launched 63 companies, creating more than 13 000 jobs and generating more than USD200 million in follow-on venture capital investments – most of which is new capital into the state.

A number of university-industry linkages have enhanced economic growth and promoted economic development in the region, including initiatives in non-woven textiles, electronics, bio-pharmaceuticals, advanced medical care, housing and small business development. The establishment of the 'Centennial Campus' for private sector-university collaboration has played a major role in enhancing regional economic development. A national model for partnerships among business, government and the university, more than 130 companies, government agencies, and North Carolina state research and academic units reside on the Centennial Campus.

In summary, with respect to university-industry linkages and its role in promoting economic development, three features stand out in the relationship between higher education (as exemplified by NCSU) on the one hand, and the private sector and government on the other:

- Innovation: A culture of innovation has been fostered that encourages and rewards intellectual leadership on the part of both staff and students, through, inter alia, pioneering new methods of instruction, and a highly relevant curricula in a multidisciplinary academic approach.
- Research: The institution is research-focused and deeply engaged in knowledge discovery and application driven by its disciplines.
- Partnerships: There are active and unique partnerships with business, government, community, other universities and schools. By leveraging these partnerships, along with its own Centennial Campus and proximity to and association with the world-famous Research Triangle Park, the university has succeeded in creating a dynamic and rewarding learning environment.

Funding

On budgetary matters, the UNCGA system negotiates with the state governor and the legislature on behalf of all 16 institutions, which are not supposed to negotiate independently. This arrangement has been very beneficial to the UNC system: the state of North Carolina puts more money into higher education per capita than any other state that is capable of similar economies of scale. Notwithstanding this level of centralisation in dealing with the state of North Carolina, the individual institutions run their affairs completely independently within the bounds of some constraints set by the UNCGA.

The funding mechanisms/arrangements vary from specific contracts, work through sales and services agreements, memoranda of understanding (a legal understanding between a unit in the North Carolina state higher education system and a unit in the state government), legislative special funding, and consortial arrangements across either a group of institutions and/or institutions and non-profit agencies.

The different colleges and universities handle research, research grants and their relationships with the private sector in their own ways (although the UNCGA may place some reasonable and not very restrictive constraints on them). Committees are not as important as they are, for example, in South Africa, the United Kingdom or Australia. Funds that come from the private sector may not have to be vetted and approved by the UNCGA, but would have to be by each campus administration. At NCSU, for example, there are vice-chancellors for research; extension, engagement, and economic development; and university advancement. These individuals, who report to the chief executive officer or chancellor, are supposed to champion and facilitate developments in their fields. They have executive responsibility and are not hidebound by committees. There are some committees (e.g. to consider research leave applications), but they tend to be small working groups. The system thus attempts to minimise the danger of 'bureaucratic blockages' to the efficient running of the institution. At the academic management level, moreover, there are numerous faculty committees and sub-committees.

Identifying future challenges in higher education: The UNC Tomorrow Commission
In 2006, the North Carolina higher education system established a multi-stakeholder commission called the UNC Tomorrow Commission to investigate and report on the challenges facing higher education and the state. The findings of the Commission are relevant to developing countries to the extent that the challenges identified are precisely those facing this group of countries as well.

The UNC Tomorrow Commission acknowledges the importance of higher education, first, for economic development (e.g. it makes representations on 'global readiness' of the higher education system, and on economic transformation), and second, for sustainable development more broadly (e.g. in its concern for health and environmental issues). In other words, it is recognised that the challenges of higher education go beyond 'pure education issues' to those relating both to globalisation and the local environment. With regard to public school education, the Commission recognises the need for the UNC system to play a greater role in improving the quantity, quality and distribution of teachers, helping to address the shortage of science and maths teachers, and strengthening efforts to help schools to reduce drop-out and repetition rates. In other words, there is an important role for public universities in helping to raise the quality of school education, a key factor for the success of higher education.

Furthermore, the issue of improving public education is extremely important for both North Carolina and countries in Africa. It should be noted that North Carolina has for many years been a national leader in per capita support for higher education, but not in per capita support for public school education. The UNCGA has pursued a policy of very low tuition fees (compared to other states in the United States) on the basis that this was necessary to sustain student access in the state. This policy has proven successful in maintaining the historically high per capita support for the UNC system. However, this policy has not provided greater student access/participation compared to other states. In part this is because North Carolina has invested more funds in the university system and fewer funds in state-based student aid than other states, and in part because of low graduation rates and inadequate high school preparation in the (relatively) under-funded public school system. Thus there has been some criticism that North Carolina, similar to many developing countries, may be over-investing in higher education and under-investing in public education relative to the needs of the state.

The case for differentiating the higher education system in order to better meet society's needs is strong. A major challenge to all systems of higher education in today's globalised environment is 'mission creep', in which all institutions seek to become 'world-class' universities at increasing cost to the state and to needed institutional diversity. As described earlier, Finland, for example, has more effectively limited the effects of 'mission creep' and encouraged greater institutional diversity in meeting national needs by maintaining clearly differentiated university and polytechnic sectors. The state of California has a community college system, similar to North Carolina's, as well as a separately administered university system and a state college system (now called universities, but limited in graduate education and research). In this sense, the UNC system structure is a weakness because it combines 16 different types of institutions into one system and attempts to develop common policies for the entire system. It also imposes another layer of very costly bureaucracy (the UNCGA), whose benefits to the state are mostly unclear. Within the system there is evidence of 'mission creep' by the lesser known universities/colleges. There is also frustration among the two internationally recognised universities (UNC Chapel Hill and NCSU) because of their limited managerial and financial autonomy as a consequence of the existence of the UNC system office.

> The case for differentiating the higher education system in order to better meet society's needs is strong

***

In the remaining three sections of this chapter, the key findings of the three case studies discussed above are outlined. The first section describes the role of higher education in economic development in each case; the second summarises the common features and differences in the three regions; and the third attempts to distil some possible implications for African countries.

Synthesis

The role of higher education in economic development

Finland

The Finnish experience demonstrates that higher education influences economic development in several ways.

First, higher education produces 'human capital' through its education and training function in the form of graduates in high numbers and of high quality. These graduates contribute specifically to economic development and to overall development (including its social dimension) in a number of ways, for example, through their contribution to research, education (as teachers) and to economic growth directly (e.g. engineers).

Second, the higher education institutions place a strong emphasis on research and development, and both the universities and the polytechnics in different ways play a critical role in the R&D function – and in the innovation system as a whole.

Third, higher education is very closely linked to national development policy, particularly regional development policy. The higher education system of universities and polytechnics covers the whole country and within this dual system, the universities are charged with academic research and education based on it, and the polytechnics with higher education geared to the world of work and research which serves education, the world of work and regional development.

Fourth, the higher education system forms the basis for a regionally comprehensive innovation system which is regarded in the country as being critical for growth and development. In this system, universities and polytechnics are seen to be key components.

Fifth, the higher education institutions play a key role with industry in enhancing regional development through their support and research role in such initiatives as the Centres of Expertise programme and the technology/science parks.

Sixth, recent research has shown the value of equity in stimulating growth and development. The commitment of the Finnish government to equity in general and of the higher education system in particular, must have been an important contributor to the high rates of economic growth experienced in Finland in recent decades.

Seventh, the high success rates of graduates from the higher education system in the labour market in terms of both employment and earnings points both to the high levels of 'external efficiency' of the higher education system and to its clear role in promoting economic growth.

South Korea

The South Korean experience also shows the critical influence of higher education on economic development but there are some fundamental differences compared to the situation in Finland.

First, the South Korean education system has also responded well to the basic educational needs of the population and was successful in delivering the human resources required for South Korea's industrialisation efforts. However, the rapid quantitative expansion of the higher education system appears to have led to a lowering of quality, and limited diversity and relevance. In that policy context, the higher educational institutions have not been able to provide the quality of human resources to flexibly meet the changing demand in a knowledge-based economy.

Second, in South Korea, strategic partnerships and connections, along with institutional and organisational structures that govern such partnerships, among knowledge-producing institutions such as corporations, universities and research institutions, are weak.

Third, universities have focused on the traditional mission of training scholars and the leaders of society. They have remained relatively passive in the practical application of knowledge and failed to respond effectively to job market realities. The universities have not succeeded in specialising in a manner that reflects the uniqueness of local industry and culture – consequently, their role as a centre for creating and disseminating knowledge in the local community has remained weak.

Fourth, South Korea has a large pool of highly educated workers. More than 80% of high-school graduates go on to higher education, but there is a problem of imbalance between academic fields. Professional schools, including law and medical schools, are much preferred to the science and engineering faculties. There is, however, an increasing demand for college students who will develop the core competencies needed in the knowledge-based economy of the 21st century. It is evident though that Korean universities are not improving college students' competencies in critical thinking, communication, self-motivated learning, leadership and problem-solving.

However, there is increasing evidence that the South Korean education system is starting to respond to these demands. Primary and secondary education now focus more on excellence and creativity than on generality, and some components of the tertiary education system (e.g. the National University of Seoul) provide competitive, high-quality education and research. The expanded private system is expected to provide greater coherence with the needs of the labour market. In that context, South Korea's education policy and system have been moving forward from the past industrial model toward a knowledge-based model since the mid-1990s.

Fifth, as a sign of its intention to promote restructuring for efficiency, the government announced a University Restructuring Plan in 2004. The key objectives of the plan are to:

- Lay the foundation for improving the quality of higher education beyond the growth in quantity
- Improve the efficiency of tertiary education investment
- Develop human resources that meet the needs of society, and
- Support development of Korean universities to become world-class institutions.

Although it is too early to tell whether the government's university-restructuring initiatives will succeed, a fair number of colleges and universities are in the process of restructuring and downsizing. In 2005, eight national colleges and universities in local provinces were consolidated into four universities, and 38 higher education institutions announced their intention to downsize their enrolments by about 10% over the next three years. Nevertheless, it remains to be seen whether the higher education institutions will be able to become more distinctive.

Sixth, the South Korean experience of economic and parallel educational development is a classic example of the East Asian experience with catch-up industrial development. Universities have played a very special role in East Asian development – not as drivers of innovation but as shapers of human capital formation. Throughout this past half-century, universities were at the forefront in training large numbers of highly skilled graduates, who could be employed successfully by domestic firms seeking to enter global industries, by multinational corporations, and by the public institutions steering the economy's industrial development. The foundation for this role played by the universities and newly established polytechnics was the steadily rising rate of adult literacy and numeracy, and the high quality of primary and secondary education. This is precisely what occurred in South Korea.

By contrast, the public research institutions (PRIs) played the role of technology capture agencies and technology diffusion managers, going abroad to seek the technologies needed by local firms and building capabilities in those technologies which the PRIs passed across to the private sector as rapidly as possible. These institutes worked closely with domestic firms, developing their capacities to become technologically sophisticated players in their own right. PRIs drove the development of national innovative capacity in East Asian economies as they gradually moved from catching up and imitation to fast-follower innovation. For example, in South Korea in the 1970s, President Park recruited, at enormous cost, the finest Korean scientists living abroad to establish the now foremost PRI in the country, the Korean Institute of Science and Technology (KAIST). KAIST very quickly became the leading agency in the country for technology capture and transfer.

In keeping with the latecomer model of development, the East Asian economies such as South Korea never saw universities as agents of innovation – at least not during their half-century of accelerated catching up. Rather, they saw universities as agents of human capital formation – that is, advanced training institutions.

Although universities played the role of human capital formation institutions, the actual task of leveraging technology and diffusing it to the private sector was allocated to PRIs. They emerged as the central and defining institutions of the East Asian catch-up experience. In recent years, especially since 2002, there is evidence that universities such as Seoul National University are beginning to play an increasingly important role in R&D.

In summary, the current reforms in Korean higher education relating to quality, differentiation and relevance, and the attempts to stimulate research capacity in the universities, are designed to enhance Korean human resource capacity to respond more creatively and fully to the challenges of innovation and the increasingly globalised and knowledge-based economy of the 21st century.

North Carolina

Even though North Carolina is located in the richest (in terms of total wealth) and most powerful country, its education system is the least developed of the three case studies considered here. The schooling system faces many developing country-type challenges, particularly with regard to access and quality. Participation in higher education is relatively low compared to Finland and South Korea, and highly inequitable in terms of race, class and region.

Nevertheless, there are several features of the North Carolina higher education system that are important with respect to its impact on development.

First, the state plays an important role in funding and promoting engagement between higher education institutions and the private sector.

Second, there is a high level of productive engagement between higher education institutions and the private sector, particularly in response to changing economic conditions.

Third, there are very good linkages between universities and other post-secondary institutions (such as community colleges), particularly with regard to ensuring a clear division of roles and articulation.

Fourth, the community colleges address two basic challenges, that of workforce/skills development, and providing access to those unable to attend universities in the first instance.

Fifth, the North Carolina universities, particularly the two leading institutions, have developed productive linkages with the private sector to enhance economic development through R&D and cultivating a culture of innovation.

Sixth, there is increasing recognition that universities can play a greater role in improving the quantity, quality and distribution of teachers, help address the shortage of science and maths teachers, and strengthen efforts to help schools to reduce drop-out and repetition rates. In other words, there is an important role for public universities in helping to raise the quality of school education, a key factor for the success of higher education.

Common threads and differences

Table 2 provides a summary of the similarities and differences in the findings relating to higher education and economic development in the three international case studies.

Table 2
Higher education and economic development in Finland, South Korea and North Carolina – common threads and differences

Criterion	Finland	South Korea	North Carolina
Access to schooling	High	High	Varies by region, race and class
Quality of schooling	High	High	Varies by race, region and class
Participation in higher education	High	High	High
Differentiation in higher education	Clear differentiation between universities and polytechnics	Strong differentiation between colleges and universities	Clear differentiation between colleges and universities, but not between universities
Commitment to equity in higher education			
Gender	Strong	Moderate	Moderate
Class	Strong	Moderate	Weak
Region	Strong	Moderate	Weak
Linking education to economic development	Strong	Strong	Weak in policy terms, but strong in practice
Public funding of higher education	High	Low	Moderate
Research and innovation			
Expenditure	High public and private	High private	High private and university
Institutional arrangements for distribution of funds and coordination of policy	Strong, between government, higher education institutions, and private sector	Weak	Strong between private sector and universities
Role of higher education	Strong	Weak	Strong
Higher education–industry linkages	Strong	Weak, but improving	Strong
Quality of higher education	High	Moderate	Varies from excellent to very moderate
Labour market responsiveness	Very good	Good	Very good

Synthesis

Some possible implications for African countries

This section summarises the possible implications for African countries from the three case studies.

1. Linking economic and education planning

The Finnish system clearly illustrates the benefits of maintaining a close link between economic and education planning. This has been particularly true since policy decisions were taken to focus on the development of a knowledge economy. The link between higher education and national development has been a particularly close one. A feature of economic policy has been targeted intervention in the industrialisation process with far-reaching implications for specific categories of outputs from the higher education system, such as engineers, scientists and teachers.

The South Korean system clearly illustrates the benefits of maintaining a close link between economic and education planning. The government has been unashamedly interventionist in both sectors to promote overall social and economic development, with profound consequences over the past 40 years.

In North Carolina there is no formal state, government-induced planning in either the education or economic sectors. However, there is a close working relationship between the education and economic bureaucracies in the state government, the private business sector and public higher education institutions, to achieve the education and training as well as research and innovation objectives necessary for economic and broader development.

2. Building higher education on a sound foundation of high-quality, equitable schooling

The Finnish model also shows how crucial high-quality schooling is for the development of a high-quality higher education system. An important aspect of social equity in Finland is the system of comprehensive education. The high quality of schooling provides a sound platform for a good quality, efficient higher education system.

The Korean model shows how crucial high-quality schooling is for the development of a high-quality higher education system. While there are serious questions about overall quality in the Korean higher education system, largely as a consequence of the rapid quantitative expansion, the higher education system has nevertheless been able to provide a large quantity of human capital to contribute to the country's rapid industrialisation efforts since the 1960s.

In North Carolina, it is evident that the success of higher education is critically dependent on improving public school education. This implies increasing access and equity, and improving the quality and efficiency of education at all levels. Unlike in Finland and South Korea, quality of schooling (and of higher education) in North Carolina varies substantially across the region.

3. High participation rates with institutional differentiation

All three systems have some of the highest post-school tertiary education participation ratios in the world. All three, albeit in different ways, provide post-school education at both the middle- and high-end skills levels. This is done through combining high participation with differentiation. In the one approach, the two higher education sub-sectors have fundamentally different roles. The polytechnics are seen as institutions which prepare their students for practical work, while the mission of the universities is more academic and has a theoretical and research orientation. However, the polytechnics also undertake research related to the world of work.

Polytechnics in Finland also play a broader, community-based education role. As with the community colleges in the United States, the polytechnics are involved in educational extension services, such as adult education. The polytechnic thus has multiple roles, including vocational education, adult education and vocational education research.

In South Korea, there is clear role differentiation between colleges and universities. The former exist to prepare middle-level human resources and technicians. The universities, on the other hand, are required to produce high-level skills, including potential researchers for the private sector and public research institutions. Recent years have seen the start of some institutional differentiation within the university sector, with a few institutions, such as Seoul National University, playing an increasing role in research in addition to their education and training functions.

In North Carolina, the post-secondary sector, including universities and community colleges, is appropriately differentiated to cater to the differing needs of the population and the economy. However, there is little differentiation within the university sector, with almost all of them aspiring to becoming 'world-class' research institutions.

Differentiation within an elite higher education system contributes to inequality and high-level skills shortages in the knowledge economy, while differentiation within a high participation system reduces inequality by providing large numbers from a cross spectrum of students with wide-ranging capabilities to prepare for a range of skills and jobs.

4. Strong state steering

The state can play a dominant role in the development of an effective higher education system. The Finnish system demonstrates, for example, that the state through its role, inter alia, in funding, can ensure the development of a higher education system that is appropriate to the country's needs.

In South Korea, providing high-quality schooling on an equitable basis has meant that fewer public resources have been available for public higher education. The development of a largely private higher education system has produced some far-reaching consequences in terms of deficiencies relating to labour market responsiveness and in relation to the general quality of outputs, particularly from that component of the system. In essence, in

South Korea, the state has chosen to play a much more dominant role in the development of the schooling system compared to higher education, which is largely private.

In North Carolina, the role of the state in higher education is that of a facilitator and an important funding source. As a facilitator it has driven important partnerships with the private business sector and higher education institutions.

5. Different roles for private higher education

In all three case studies the role of private higher education institutions varies. In Finland, given the strong and committed role of the state to providing higher education, until recently there has been no role for the private sector. In North Carolina, the private sector is an important provider of higher education, at both the university and college levels, ideally complementing state provision. In South Korea, there has been and continues to be a high priority given to investment in high-quality schooling at all levels. As a consequence, the state has relatively few resources for investment in higher education. This has led to the development of a dominant private sector in higher education both in terms of institutions and enrolments.

6. Higher education linked to regional development

Higher education can play an important role in regional development. In Finland, universities and polytechnics spread over the entire country work in collaboration with one another and with local government and business to ensure greater equity in regional development. South Korea is now addressing regional development through such initiatives as the New University for Regional Innovation. In North Carolina, equitable regional development has not been a priority. Even though higher education institutions are spread throughout the country, those outside the major cities tend invariably to be of poorer quality.

7. Strong cooperation and networks

Cooperation and consensus is a key factor in policy-making and implementation. The Finnish system is characterised by a high degree of consensus-building and cooperation between stakeholders in the higher education system, including higher education institutions, government, public funding agencies and the private sector. This has been a key factor in stimulating efficiency and effectiveness in the distribution of resources and the development of appropriate education and research outcomes.

Appropriate institutional arrangements created through legislation also help in the achievement of efficient and effective outcomes in higher education. The Finnish model illustrates clearly the value of appropriate institutional arrangements in a number of areas – whether it is with a view to developing consensus in strategic policy-making (e.g. Science and Technology Policy Council), ensuring efficient resource allocation (funding agencies), or designing a strong innovation system (private sector/government/higher education institutions).

In South Korea, the hand of government is clearly 'visible' in all components of the education system, including oversight of the private sector. Historically, an important network has been that between the relevant government ministries, the public research institutions and

Synthesis

the large private sector companies (chaebols) with respect to research and development. Increasingly today, universities, particularly the large public institutions, are becoming an important fourth component of this group as they develop their R&D capacity. Second, important linkages are developing directly between industry and universities, particularly through initiatives such as the Industry–Academia Collaboration. Finally, the third set of networks that is developing somewhat belatedly is that between universities, industry and regional governments in initiatives such as the Regional Innovation Committee and the New University for Regional Innovation. In summary, there has been a dramatic change in the nature of the higher education networks from one historically dominated by central government to one in which the private business sector and regional governments are starting to play an increasingly important role. Such initiatives are beginning to address both the role of universities in R&D and also the challenge of regional equity in the quality of higher education institutions.

The North Carolina case study shows how effective relationships can be developed between the higher education system on the one hand, and government, the private business sector and civil society broadly on the other, in order to promote economic, social and environmental development. None of these relationships have been legislated, but they have come about through a common commitment to the development of the state.

8. Responsive to labour market demand

In Finland, the higher education system must be able to meet the demands of the labour market. An important feature of the Finnish higher education system is its relatively high level of success in meeting the demands of its labour market. An important factor here has been the role of the state in providing disproportionate resources for scarce skills.

In South Korea, it is evident that the higher education system has, to a great extent, not been able to produce the required quality of outputs for a knowledge-based economy. There is a large divergence between what employers are seeking of university graduates and their skills base. This is possibly the most important reason why South Korea has yet to make the leap to a growth pattern in which sectors demanding high-quality educated labour (the service sector generally through the information technology, finance and other sub-sectors) are dominating the composition of GDP.

There are several lessons here. First, quality has inevitably been compromised by the rapid expansion of the system in a very short time. Second, expansion was accompanied by very little institutional differentiation, especially at the university level. Third, it was expected that the private sector-dominated system would be better able to provide human resources in line with the needs of the economy, but this has clearly not happened. The ability of the government to 'steer' the system with appropriate incentives has not been possible in a system dominated by privately-financed institutions.

The North Carolina experience shows that the higher education system should be sufficiently flexible to respond to changing labour market conditions. In the absence of state planning, the higher education system has, nevertheless, been able to respond reasonably well to changing labour market demand patterns of an increasingly sophisticated economy.

9. Positive role higher education plays in development

In Finland, higher education is closely linked to economic and national development through its education and training role (the provider of 'human capital') and in its varied and wide-ranging roles in research and innovation.

Korean government higher education policy for most of the past four decades was to ensure that universities produced human capital for growth and development. The role of higher education institutions in research and innovation was minimal – the role of technology capture, transfer and development was left initially to the public research institutions and then to private companies. This model is largely the one that prevails in Africa; that is, universities are largely the providers of human capital (graduates) with very little research and innovation taking place in higher education institutions. This raises the vexing question of why African countries have not been able to match the economic growth and development record of South Korea in the post-Second World War era. One possible answer here lies in the failure of African countries to provide adequate access to good quality schooling.

In North Carolina, higher education is recognised as important for economic and broader social and environmental development (in other words, sustainable development). This is particularly so in a rapidly globalising world where patterns of economic development are no longer homogenous as in the 19th and early 20th centuries. The North Carolina case study also illustrates the numerous challenges relating to, inter alia, access, equity and quality, that need to be addressed if a more equitable pattern of development is to be attained.

Box 1
Key implications for African countries

1. Linking economic and education planning
2. Building higher education on a sound foundation of high-quality, equitable schooling
3. High participation rates with institutional differentiation
4. Strong state steering
5. Different roles for private higher education
6. Higher education linked to regional development
7. Strong cooperation and networks
8. Responsive to labour market demand
9. Positive role higher education plays in development

In conclusion, it would be easy to dismiss the findings of this study as being irrelevant for African countries given that all three case studies are from the rich, industrialised world. There are, however, important reasons why African policy-makers should take note of the importance of higher education for development generally, and for economic development specifically. First, the relationship between higher education and economic development is incontrovertible. Through its education and training, and research functions, higher education can enable countries both to raise economic growth rates and increase participation in the knowledge-based economy. Second, in the globalising world, poor countries need not base their economies entirely on the production of primary commodities and manufactured goods requiring skills provided by primary and secondary education. It is possible for developing/poor countries to focus at the same time also on the production of value-adding goods and services requiring skills provided by the higher education system. The advantage of the latter strategy is that it can raise growth rates much more rapidly, enabling, inter alia, the government to expand the provision of economic and social services to those trapped in poverty.

Synthesis

CHAPTER 2
Finland

Education and the economy

There are several features of the Finnish political economy that are crucial to an understanding of the relationship between higher education and economic development. Foremost amongst these factors is a longstanding and unshakeable commitment to equity in all its forms (such as gender, region and socio-economic status). Second, as a strong proponent of the Nordic welfare state model, the role of the Finnish government in higher education is all-embracing and is reflected, inter alia, in the high levels of resourcing for the sector, and in the commitment to both the education and research roles of higher education. Third, there is a strong commitment to consensus-building in general on the part of all the social partners (government, private business and civil society).

The Finnish economy has undergone dramatic transformation in the last 50 years. Two distinct periods are discernible: the immediate post-Second World War period during which the economy became closely linked to that of the Soviet Union, and the period following the collapse of the Soviet Union in the early 1990s. In the latter period, Finland suffered a severe depression and, amongst other things, the government had to step in to save the banking sector.

At the time of the 1990s crisis, the Finnish government was faced with an economic policy choice of either following the New Zealand 'free market' model or the Nordic welfare state model. It chose the latter. Key to the development of economic policy was determining what would be the national strength of the economy. It was at this time that the government chose to invest in the knowledge economy through an extensive funding programme in the fields of high technology and knowledge-based industries. In line with this economic policy decision, the role of higher education assumed much greater importance in the 1990s.

The Finnish economy has historically relied on the utilisation of its large forests. After the Second World War, Finland created a metal and engineering industry alongside the traditional forest industry. In recent decades, Finland's success in building a globally-orientated electronics industry has dramatically diversified the production structure. There are currently three almost equally important export sectors in the Finnish economy: electronics and electrotechnical goods, metal and engineering products, and forest industry products. The chemical industry is the fourth-largest export sector.

Beginning in the 1990s, the government took definitive steps to stimulate the development of knowledge through promoting information and communication technologies (ICT) and innovation. The process by which information and know-how became Finland's key resource is also reflected in the rapid increase in research and development (R&D) spending. In 2004, R&D represented 3.5% of the gross national product (GNP) – high by international and Organisation for Economic Cooperation and Development (OECD) standards. The communications sector has made substantial input into innovation. The ICT companies also influence innovation in other sectors, and facilitate intercompany R&D collaboration as well as cooperation with the scientific community.

Exports from Finland have grown at an extremely rapid rate since the early 1990s and export growth has been a key element in economic restructuring. Whereas in 1990 exports accounted for 23% of gross domestic product (GDP), by 2001 this figure had soared to 42% (MoE 2005: 13). Growth has been made possible by competitive prices and expertise in high-tech production and product development.

Finland's GDP increased 1.5 times between 1985 and 2001, even though it decreased dramatically between 1990 and 1994.[1] The large overall increase in GDP during the last 20 years coincided with the expansion and diversification of the higher education system.

The rapid rise in the educational level of the labour force is reflected in the great differences in the level of education between different age groups. Among the employed, the age group with the highest educational level is 25–34-year-olds – about 40% of whom had a tertiary degree in 1997 (MoE 2005: 15). The corresponding figure for the 55–64 age group was 18%. Thus the educational level of those leaving the labour force is low, while those entering the labour force are highly educated.

As the economy was transformed, so was the higher education system. In the 1960s and 1970s, the Ministry of Education (MoE) was very strong relative to the higher education institutions, with the latter having very little autonomy and their budgets controlled, leaving the university to be seen as an extension of the civil service.

The mid-1980s OECD review was highly critical of higher education policy and this report was taken very seriously by the Finnish government, in particular, the relationship between the government and universities. In 1988–1989, the Development Law for higher education was passed and the principles of the new relationship between government and higher education institutions were defined, providing a framework for self-regulation and increased autonomy, but also increased accountability, for example, around outputs/ outcomes, expenditures, and quality and evaluation through a quality assurance system. During the 1990s, the infrastructure and capacity of the higher education institutions for self-regulation was established.

In summary, Finland's national objective is sustainable and balanced social and economic development. High employment, productivity and competitiveness are key factors. A high quality higher education system and measures to increase research and technological development play a significant part in attempts to attain the country's national development goals. As Castells and Himanen (2001: 115) point out:

> *Spatial clustering and organizational networking of knowledge-based industries have been critical sources of productivity and competitiveness... the Finnish experience shows the synergy that can be created from networking between different levels of government in the design of developmental public policy.*

The higher education system

The main characteristics of Finland's higher education system are as follows (MoE 2005):

- A comprehensive, dual-sector higher education system, comprising 20 universities and 29 polytechnics, spread geographically across the whole country.
- A high participation rate in higher education in general, including high proportions of female and mature-age students.
- The stability of the higher education system: the structure is transparent and the functions of the two sectors are clearly defined.
- The public nature of the system, with the student population attending fee-free public institutions.
- A relatively high proportion of funding for higher education institutions is drawn from the public purse.
- A high proportion of research is conducted in public research institutes.
- Private investment in research has increased more rapidly than public investment during the past few decades.
- The relative share of funding of university research from external sources has increased.
- A marked quantitative expansion in research training, combined with the introduction of a graduate school system.
- A well-integrated higher education system with few barriers related to the recognition of credit transfer between institutions.
- Graduates from both first degrees and the PhD programmes are relatively 'old' at time of graduation. Those with higher education qualifications have relatively low rates of unemployment.
- Relatively few foreign students.
- A decentralised admission system for universities.

The main ongoing policy directions of the MoE can be summarised as follows (MoE 2005):

- Strengthening cooperation between higher education institutions and forming new consortia between universities and polytechnics.
- Intensifying research and development in polytechnics as well as their cooperation with regional organisations.

- Rationalising higher education provision by reducing the number of providers or by merging institutions.
- The unifying of the system of external decision-making for polytechnics.
- The standardisation of the system for external oversight and funding of the polytechnic sector. Polytechnics receive much of their funding from the MoE, but major oversight is the responsibility of bodies such as regional or city councils.
- Changing existing polytechnic funding mechanisms by introducing a more stable, measurable and incentive-based system.
- Strengthening the development of internationally-competitive universities.
- Intensifying quality assurance systems.
- Continuing to develop a university funding formula based more on the attainment of results and on institutional outputs.
- Shortening the time elapsed between the completion of secondary education and the commencement of tertiary education.
- The university sector will be developed into a worldclass system in Finland's areas of strength, one which will continuously generate new research openings and initiatives. The polytechnics will be developed as regional forces. The higher education system will not be further expanded.
- The higher education institutions will have to combine their resources into larger entities and boost networking, management and impact analysis. Universities will improve their international competitiveness by raising their profiles and by investing in high-quality research across disciplinary borders and research personnel of an internationally-recognised high standard. The organisations with oversight over polytechnics, together with the MoE, will have to ensure that polytechnics are of a sufficient size, are multidisciplinary in range, and invest in high-standard education which is responsive to regional work and life needs.

Finnish universities are governed by the Universities Act (1997) which assigns four missions to universities: to promote free research; to promote scientific and artistic education; to provide higher education based on research; and to educate students to serve their country and humanity.

The Finnish polytechnic system was set up over a period of ten years, which comprised a pilot phase and a subsequent stage in which the operations were given their final form. In the reform, vocational colleges joined forces and formed larger entities, upgrading their education to the tertiary level. The first polytechnics gained a permanent status in August 1996 and the last five in August 2000.

Polytechnics are professionally-orientated higher education institutions. In addition to their education role, polytechnics conduct applied R&D which serves teaching and the work life. The polytechnic network covers the entire country from the north to south and from east to west, catering for the speakers of both national languages (Finnish and Swedish).

Polytechnic degrees are Bachelor-level tertiary degrees with a professional emphasis and take 3.5 to 4.5 years to complete. The main aim of the polytechnic programmes is to provide professional competence. The largest fields are engineering, business and healthcare.

The polytechnics gained a permanent status in legislation passed in 2003. According to the Polytechnics Act, these institutes provide professional education, support professional development, conduct applied R&D which supports regional development, and offer adult education.

The dual structure has several special characteristics:

- The two higher education sub-sectors are fundamentally different. The polytechnics are seen as institutions which prepare their students for practical work, while the mission of universities is more academic and has a theoretical and research orientation.
- The degrees and degree programmes are different in polytechnics and universities. The universities have a two-cycle degree structure (Bachelor-Master) while the polytechnics have so far had only one level of degree (Bachelor). A three-year pilot of postgraduate polytechnic degrees was launched in 2002.
- The model of administration is different in the universities and the polytechnics. The universities are maintained by the state, while the polytechnics are run by municipalities, joint municipal bodies and foundations. These maintaining organisations (and external partners) have a stronger role in their administration, and sometimes also a more direct impact on their operations.
- The administrative structure and staff categories of universities are largely geared to support research, while polytechnics are mainly institutes of teaching, with fewer research-related tenures.
- The funding systems are geared to support the special mission of each sector. In universities, external funding is largely targeted to research. At first, polytechnics obtained funds for the development of their basic operations and later, for teaching and the regional service functions.

Research has indicated that the dual ideology has been well received both by the labour market and by students seeking admission to tertiary education. The more professionally-orientated candidates apply to a polytechnic and the more theoretically disposed choose the university. This clear division is also reflected in the opinions expressed by employers. With their distinct profile, polytechnic graduates compete for the same jobs as university graduates. Moreover, there is consensus in Finland concerning the respective missions of the polytechnics and universities.

As far as the higher education system is concerned, the dominant feature is the dual or binary system of universities and polytechnics.

In Finland, the dual system is thus held to be clearly differentiated in terms of:

- The nature of the degree structure

Finland

- The model of governance and administration: state compared with a municipality, joint municipal bodies or foundations
- The profile of funding related to the differentiated mission, and the different priority ascribed to research, and
- The internal cultures, organisational and management practices which, on the one hand, reflect a collegial model (universities) and, on the other, a more managerial/ corporatist model (polytechnics).

Research and development

In the Finnish economy there is a strong emphasis on R&D and the universities – as well as the polytechnics, to a lesser extent – play an important role in the R&D function.

In 2003, R&D expenditure was EUR5 billion, equivalent to 3.5% of GDP. Of this amount, the higher education sector expenditure (universities, polytechnics and university central hospitals) was EUR976 million, or about 19% of overall expenditure. The business sector accounted for 70% and the public sector (mainly state research institutes) 10%. At 1% of GDP, public R&D funding is amongst the highest in the world (the European Union average is 0.77%) (MoE 2005).

Table 3
State R&D expenditure by institution type, Finland

Institution	% of state budget
Universities	26
Academy of Finland	14
Tekes	28
State research institutes	16
University central hospitals	2
Other	13

Source: MoE (2005)

In 2005, the MoE allocated EUR640 million to research, which represents 40% of all state R&D funding. Most of this sum was allocated to universities and the Academy of Finland (which funds further higher education research on a competitive basis). Research expenditure accounted for almost 11% of the total expenditure in the MoE administrative sector (MoE 2005).

In 2003 external funding represented 77% of research funding in polytechnics and 49% in universities (MoE 2005). The foremost sources of research income for polytechnics were European Union funds, domestic businesses and MoE project funding. The primary external sources of financing for universities were the Academy of Finland (research funding) and the National Technology Agency Tekes (technology funding).

At the time of writing, funding for R&D at higher education institutions was above EUR1 billion (MoE 2005). This is 20% of the total national R&D expenditure and about twice as much as all other public support for research combined. The universities get the largest share of this, while hospitals and polytechnics each receive less than one-tenth of the universities' share. However, R&D expenditures at the polytechnics have grown rapidly in recent years, from EUR27 million in 1999 to EUR67 million in 2003. This is consistent with a changing role of the polytechnics which used to be viewed as teaching institutions only. Today R&D activities are included in their formal obligations. This might provide a major boost for research-based quality education in the polytechnics, but it is a problem that the basic (core) funding for research in these institutions does not yet match their ambitious intentions.

In Finland the national science, technology and innovation policies are formulated by the Science and Technology Policy Council, which is chaired by the Prime Minister. The Council is responsible for the strategic development and coordination of Finnish science and technology policy. It advises the government and its ministries on questions relating to science and technology, the general development of scientific research and researcher training, and Finnish participation in international scientific and technological cooperation.

The national authorities primarily responsible for science and technology policy are the MoE and the Ministry of Employment and the Economy (MoEE). The MoE is in charge of matters relating to researcher training, science policy and the Academy of Finland. The MoEE deals with matters relating to industrial and technology policies, the National Technology Agency (Tekes) and the Technical Research Centre of Finland (VTT). Nearly 80% of government R&D funding is channelled through these two ministries.

The Academy of Finland, the Finnish research council organisation, takes care of the central research administration and finances a major part of university research. The Academy has four research councils, appointed for three-year terms, each financing research in their disciplines. Another important task for the Academy is to evaluate research. Public funding for technology and development is channelled through Tekes, which also plays a major part in the external funding of the universities.

Research support for higher education institutions is divided into core funding and competitive funding. The former is well suited for long-term infrastructure development in the higher education institutions, while the latter is usually of a time-limited nature and is much less useful for the long-term development of institutional infrastructure. Most of the competitive funding is provided by the Finnish Academy and Tekes, and is part of the higher education institution support that has grown most in recent years. Core funding for higher education institutions, which includes expenses for both education and research, has increased much less: in 2005 only 58% of the total support for higher education institutions was core funding, compared with 75% in 1996 (MoE 2005).

Almost half the support for R&D in higher education institutions from the Academy goes to institutions in the Helsinki area, while only 35% of the support from Tekes (covering mainly support for applied research) reaches institutions in Helsinki (MoE 2005). The fact that a high share of the research funding at higher education institutions outside Helsinki goes to applied research indicates that these higher education institutions are trying to be supportive of local technological and economic development through their research activities. This is one of the justifications for the placement of many small higher education institutions in small cities and many examples demonstrate that this regional development strategy is working effectively.

In addition to the research training that takes place in PhD and Masters programmes, the research at the higher education institutions has a strong, positive influence on the undergraduate training activities. This influence covers many aspects, from facilitating the upgrading of curricula to including the most recent developments in each field, and to allowing 'undergraduate research'; that is, students' project work at different levels. The integration of undergraduate education with research activities is today an important issue and addresses the philosophy that students should be placed at the centre of the knowledge creation process; and that knowledge creation is just as likely to take place within and with industrial partners as within the higher education institution. In a binary/ dual system, it is always an interesting question as to what the research role of the non-university sector should be, and how, if at all, it should be differentiated from that of the university sector. In general, in Finland, it might be said that the current research role of the polytechnics is perceived to encompass the following:

• Undertaking applied research/R&D based on cooperation with and funding from business, industry, public administration and sciences aimed at problem solving;
• Using research and consultancy to strengthen educational activities through underpinning scholarship and investigative, project, pedagogic and staff PhDs;
• Enhancing the economic, social and cultural development of their regions; and
• Developing peaks of excellence in a narrow range of specific institutional strengths.

During the last decade, Finland has increased its total funding for R&D considerably. Most comes from successful Finnish industries (especially Nokia, which accounts for 70% of industrial R&D expenditures). At the same time, higher education institutions have seen increasing budgets. The annual total amount spent on R&D in Finland is approaching 4% of the GNP – among the highest in the world, and second only to that of Sweden among OECD countries (MoE 2005).

Finland has rightly gained a formidable reputation for its innovative research and R&D strategies, especially those which focus on the knowledge economy and the imperative of economic regeneration and the implications of globalisation in the specific geo-political context in which Finland is located.

With research, the national agendas are following two tracks: one being the establishment of Finland as a world leader in science and technological research (fundamental and, particularly, applied research), which implies international benchmarking; the other being the deployment of R&D in the cause of economic development, especially in a regional context.

These are not in any way seen to be in conflict, but rather in a symbiotic reinforcing relationship (MoE 2005). Similarly, discussions have to be placed in the context of a binary system, where the appropriate roles of each sector are still evolving. It should be observed that there is widespread public support and concern about the need to sustain high quality research and R&D, as evidenced by the volume of government funding and initiatives across various universities, the demands of industry, and the attention of the media. This public interest is a major strength for Finnish research and for the institutions which deliver it.

The regional role of higher education

An important feature of Finnish development is the commitment to equitable regional development policies to ensure balanced national development. Higher education was appropriately decentralised in line with the evolving politically decentralised framework comprising regional councils.

A significant reform was a regional administration restructuring in 1997, in which employment and economic development centres were put in place to back up development in the regions. The regional authorities in the MoE sector are the provincial state offices, which have administered higher education matters, mainly with regard to European Union Structural Fund projects.

In the 21st century, regional development legislation was amended with the aim of devolving decision-making power to the regions in matters concerning them. Each regional council devised a four-year regional programme outlining regional development and its priorities. The regional councils prepare implementation plans for each year, the aim being that these are agreed with the central government. Although higher education does not belong to the matters governed by the regional development legislation, the region-specific implementation plans list a number of expectations regarding universities and polytechnics.

Finland's accession to the European Union in 1995 was a milestone in regional development. The Structural Funds made resources available for various regional programmes and projects and between 1995 and 1999 the MoE funded 1 170 projects, allocating a total of EUR420 million to them (MoE 2005). The European money has been especially welcome to polytechnics, which have started to take their first steps in R&D.

The government is currently preparing measures for devolving central government responsibilities to the regions. The university and polytechnic networks are already regionally decentralised and are therefore not included in this set of projected measures.

The university system grew into the present regionally comprehensive network during the 1960s and 1970s. The present 20 universities are based in 11 cities and towns, providing degree education in over 20 different localities. The aim of the regionally decentralised network is to make full use of the talent of the entire country and to produce a highly educated workforce for the needs of the growing public and business sectors.

Finland

In the 1980s, universities in Finland were increasingly seen as engines of regional development. This trend gained impetus from the improved possibilities for universities and the private sector to develop research cooperation. In the 1990s, the focus in university development was on quality. At that time, the polytechnic system was being created.

A policy decision has been taken that the university network will not be expanded further (MoE 2005). The focus is currently on enhancing the regional impact of the universities through closer cooperation and networking with business and industry and other regional players. This is a challenge, especially with regard to R&D, which can thrive only in higher education units of sufficient size and versatility. The regional impact of universities is further strengthened by the adult education network, which also covers the whole country, and the recently established university centres.

Government policy stresses the importance of cooperation within the university system and with the polytechnics. For this purpose there are new kinds of networked higher education institutions, which operate in six small towns and provide an umbrella organisation for the fairly small university units in these places with a view to diffusing research knowledge more effectively in the regions, and hence to achieving better economies of scale. Each network has a 'parent university' responsible for the operation of the centres.

The polytechnic system was created with the aim of upgrading vocationally-orientated education and catering for the changing needs of the regions and the labour market. There is at least one polytechnic in each region. Their adult education provision also covers the whole country.

Polytechnic education is currently being developed in two dimensions: as a stem network of degree education and as a service network providing extension education (e.g. adult education) and other services. The aim is to build a network in which all the degree education units are large enough to provide high-quality education and to conduct high-quality R&D in support of their regions. The structure and provision of polytechnics will be developed to enable them to become key players in their regions, supporting local municipalities, businesses and work communities and catering for local residents' self-development aspirations.

The activities of the decentralised higher education network are underpinned by the universities' and polytechnics' mutually complementary knowledge production, which in turn is based on their respective strengths. Collaboration and structural development promote the emergence of sufficiently large and diverse units needed to ensure the quality of education and research. Measures are being taken to strengthen the capacity of higher education institutions for cooperating and networking with other stakeholders in the region. Research infrastructure and support services are being developed to make quality R&D findings available in different parts of the country. Regional cooperation between universities and polytechnics in research is being boosted and their participation in regional programmes, the centre of expertise programmes, and in science and technology parks, is being promoted.

The strategic significance of knowledge is seen in the fact that many consultative bodies have been set up, mainly at the regional level, with members representing the local higher education institutions, the regional administration, local authorities and local business and industry.

Higher education and the innovation system

The Finnish higher education system forms the basis for a regionally comprehensive innovation system. The system is being developed as an entity which is both internationally competitive and responsive to regional needs.

At present universities and polytechnics are seen to be key components in the national and regional innovation systems in which they operate in close interaction with business and industry and other regional players. As a result of the current technological advances and knowledge-intensive operations, economic and social development is increasingly built on human capital. This means that the higher education institutions have a growing role in producing new knowledge and diffusing knowledge and know-how in an increasingly globalised and knowledge-based economy.

Since the 1990s, Finland has been systematically creating a national innovation system, with the aim of putting all innovation resources and products to use as speedily and effectively as possible through strong cooperation networks. The development of the innovation system is led by the Science and Technology Policy Council. Higher education institutions play a key role in the innovation system.

Universities have a special place among the regional stakeholders and have been variously called 'anchors', 'dynamos' and 'magnets' (MoE 2005). A university is an 'anchor' when it offers such research-based assets to businesses in the region that they cannot afford to move their operations, at least not all of them, elsewhere. A 'dynamo' generates new business, and a 'magnet' attracts new business. In addition to the regional mission, universities should naturally operate as strong traditional academic institutions which provide undergraduate, postgraduate and extension education.

The challenge for Finnish higher education institutions is to strike a balance between being internationally competitive in terms of teaching and research, and being sensitive to the education and research needs of their local regions.

The regional and social mission of higher education institutions is recorded in legislation. According to Section 4 of the Polytechnics Act, the mission of polytechnics is 'to provide education for professional posts and positions based on the needs of working life and its development, and on research and artistic considerations; to support individual professional development; and to conduct research and development which supports regional development and is geared to the industrial structure of the region' (MoE 2005: 37). The Act specifies that in executing its mission, the polytechnic must cooperate with industry (especially within its own region), with Finnish and foreign universities and other

Finland

educational institutions. According to the Act, no more than one-third of persons on the polytechnic board may represent business and industry.

The Universities Act of 2004 provides the third mission of universities:

> The mission of the university shall be to promote free research and scientific and artistic education, to provide higher education based on research, and to educate students to serve their country and humanity. In carrying out their mission, the universities shall interact with the surrounding society and promote the societal impact of research findings and artistic activities. (MoE 2005: 38)

The Act provides that at least one member must, and at most one-third of the university senate members may, be selected from amongst persons who do not belong to the personnel or the students of the university.

Debates concerning the third mission place strong emphasis on the need to enhance the regional impact of universities. The aim of the MoE has been to allocate additional resources to higher education institutions for their societal mission in order to prevent this from undermining their basic operations and activities.

In the division of labour between universities and polytechnics in research, universities are responsible for scientific research and education based on it, including researcher training. Doctorates are awarded only by universities. Universities also maintain most of the scientific and research infrastructure, which is funded through the university budget. Polytechnics mainly conduct R&D which caters for working-life needs, serves teaching, supports industrial life and regional development, and is based on the industrial structure of the region.

Compared with the core funding of the universities and government research establishments, the competitive funding (Academy of Finland, Tekes) has increased considerably faster. Consequently, the Academy of Finland and Tekes are the most important sources of extramural research funding in universities. Their role and the volume of funding does, however, vary between different higher education institutions.

Historically, scientific research has concentrated on universities. During the last few years the scientific role of universities has been emphasised in public debate. This is partly due to international ranking lists, which show that Finnish universities do not appear at the top of the lists. There is also a strong belief that intensifying research is the key to the economic success of the country.

At the outset polytechnics were considered mainly as teaching institutions, but their role in research has increased rapidly over the past few years and at the moment R&D is included in their statutory tasks. On the whole, however, their role in research is still relatively small. In their research role, the polytechnics have two main problems. The first is lack of basic funding for research activities; the second is lack of tradition. Genuine research communities in polytechnics are only starting to emerge. The rather scattered structure of the polytechnic system also makes it difficult for robust research environments to develop.

In summary, key success factors in the development of the innovation system include the following:

- The high quality of education at all levels
- Economic factors, especially high economic growth and the commitment to a knowledge economy
- High commitment to public and private financing of R&D
- Excellent cooperation between public and private sectors, between government departments, between higher education institutions, and between higher education institutions and the private sector
- Incentives provided by Tekes, for example, providing matching grants to private sector, and insisting that university research must be relevant
- Political consensus and citizens' support for R&D, and
- Mutual trust between science, technology and innovation players.

Finland's strategy is to ensure sustainable and balanced social and economic development. Thus far, Finland has been successful in combining economic development with the overall development of society and the environment and increasing the citizens' well-being substantially over the past few decades. In addition to the other factors, this success is grounded in the high level and quality of education of the population as well as increasingly wide-ranging development and application of knowledge and expertise.

Higher education–industry linkages

For several years now, measures have been taken to increase cooperation between higher education institutions and businesses in Finland. At the time of writing there was, however, no specific policy or programme to this end. Objectives for strengthening cooperation have been included in major strategic lines in higher education and research policy.

In its reviews, the Science and Technology Policy Council (STPC 2006) has stressed the importance of higher education institution-business cooperation. According to the Council, effective contacts and flexible cooperation have a significant effect on the spread of research findings and, with it, on the emergence of knowledge-intensive business. They further strengthen the capacity of the research system to react to changes in business life and to respond to research challenges arising from business and industry. The Council also believes that universities, research institutes and polytechnics must be developed as active and dynamic cooperation partners to business and industry with balanced development of research organisations' resources. The rules of the game in cooperation must be clarified and developed to provide incentives.

The Ministry of Education's Development Plan (2003–2008) also stresses the importance of universities' and polytechnics' cooperation with business and industry (MoE 2005). The aim is to clarify the principles underlying this cooperation and to develop the capacity of universities and polytechnics to promote the utilisation of research findings.

Tekes funding has played a great role in promoting cooperation between higher education institutions and the private sector. Tekes aims to enhance the competitiveness of manufacturing and service industries by financing and activating product development and R&D projects conducted by companies, universities, polytechnics and research institutes. It has financed the development of the technological knowledge base of universities and polytechnics and their cooperation with business and industry, with funding largely targeted at technologies and the natural sciences.

Most Academy of Finland financing is targeted at research conducted in universities and research institutes. The Academy supports researcher training by awarding grants for doctoral studies to persons active in industry. The applicant must have a postgraduate education plan approved by a university and be in an employment relationship with his or her employer for the enitre duration of doctoral studies.

The Centres of Expertise programme administered by the Ministry of the Interior encourages the regions to utilise their top expertise in order to strengthen the competitiveness of the region. There are 22 centres of expertise to this end. The programme seeks to enhance the innovation environments in regions by improving cooperation between the research sector and local business and industry. The centres of expertise are mostly run by the local science/technology park. Technology/science parks also implement the TULI (from research to business) programme financed by Tekes, which seeks to identify research-business ideas, especially in universities, polytechnics and research institutes. It offers expert services to research teams and researchers in commercialising ideas.

Universities and polytechnics offer several different support services relating to research and innovation. The most important services relate to the acquisition of R&D funding and contractual procedures. In addition, they offer careers and recruitment services to students and employers. Some higher education institutions also offer incubator services to students. Universities and polytechnics offer different extension as well as piloting and testing services to business.

Box 2 describes a case study of a mutually beneficial relationship between the country's foremost business enterprise, Nokia, and universities, research institutions and other companies.

Box 2
Nokia – a case study

What has Nokia's role been in the Finnish innovation system? The 'innovation system' here refers to the operation and interaction of universities, research institutions, other public sector organisations and private businesses which together influence the creation, diffusion and utilisation of novel know-how.

Nokia has a two-way role in the Finnish innovation system. On the one side, Nokia utilises resources from the innovation system. At the same time, the company produces innovation resources that diffuse outside the company.

In Finland, Nokia has benefited from innovation resources such as the education system, skilled labour, and Tekes R&D funding, to name a few. Similarly, Finland has reaped benefits from Nokia. The latest knowledge in the field has passed onto universities through Nokia and know-how has also spread to Nokia's partners due to its policies of networking. Nokia's international research projects have also gained in significance as a result of the company's global mode of operating.

Nokia's impact has been highly significant in terms of Finnish domestic product (around 3%), GDP growth (one-third in 2000), value of exports (close to 25%), and R&D spending (close to one-third of the total and half of total private sector R&D expenditure). On the other hand, its effect on employment is less significant. Its employees represent just over 1% of the total Finnish workforce. However, in addition to this direct effect, Nokia also has indirect influences on employment.

The significance of Nokia's position in the Finish economy is rare, even by international comparison. Although some relatively large companies exist in other small countries as well, they tend to face different circumstances. Usually, these large companies operate in low-technology industries. In Finland, Nokia operates in a technology-intensive field, which requires large R&D investments.

Tekes (the National Technology Agency) is an organisation under the Ministry of Employment and the Economy, through which the government supports and funds technology development. During the 1990s, Tekes increasingly directed funding (grants and loans) towards companies in the ICT industry. In 2001, about one-third of the funding by Tekes was targeted at the ICT industry. Nokia has also received considerable public funding for its R&D activities. As the significance of its research activity has grown, Nokia has tightened its links to universities and research institutions. As the need for highly skilled labour has also increased, Nokia has attempted to influence the level and direction of higher education.

Nokia's role in education politics became more effective as the need for qualified personnel grew in the 1990s. Through the Federation of Finnish Electrical and Electronics Industry, Nokia strived to increase the number of university starting places available in the fields of electronics, telecommunications and ICT.

Transfer of know-how to other companies
The most central channel concerning the Finnish innovation system is Nokia's cooperation with other Finnish companies. Nokia cooperates both in production and in R&D with numerous companies and in 2000 there were roughly 300 companies in Nokia's 'first tier' partner network. There were between 18 000 and 20 000 employees in these companies, who worked with products delivered to Nokia.

Most of the cooperation with companies has been aimed at production and manufacturing operations. However, over the past years cooperation has increasingly extended to operations relating to R&D.

Diffusion of know-how to universities
Nokia's cooperation with universities in Finland has mainly focused on the universities of technology and natural sciences. Through cooperation know-how has spread to various parties. The exchange of information has been two-sided; that is, in many projects the know-how has diffused from universities to Nokia and vice versa.

Nokia, even when considered more broadly, has a significant position in the Finnish information and communication cluster's innovation system. Nokia operates in the cluster as both a user and a producer of innovation resources.

Finland

Box 2 (cont.)

Regarding the innovation system, parties central to Nokia are universities, research institutions, other public sector organisations, and Nokia's suppliers and client companies. The key factors in the innovation system are the transfer of know-how, learning, and the quest for innovation. If the system functions well, the interaction of these factors reflects on the economy in the form of employment, exports, business profits and public-sector tax income.

Source: Ali-Ykro and Hermans (2002)

Higher education and quality

The main goal of public policy has been to provide equal opportunities for students from different backgrounds (such as socio-economic starting points, gender and place of residence). In the case of Finnish higher education, the government has sought to level the playing field first and foremost by means of comprehensive basic education, but also by increasing study places in higher education with a view to equal opportunity in regional terms.

Probably the most important measure taken to promote equal opportunity was the regional expansion of the university sector. With regional policy, efforts have been made to guarantee equal opportunity for young people to participate in university education, irrespective of their place of residence.

Gender equity

For almost three centuries, higher education was an overwhelmingly male pursuit in Finland. Today, women account for 54% of university students and 53% of polytechnic students. Only the field of engineering is still male-dominated. Fields such as economics and the natural sciences have equal numbers of women and men. On the other hand, education, psychology and health sciences are examples of significant female over-representation, their percentage rising as high as 80% of annual enrolment.

Equity has been an important factor in post-war educational reform. The accessibility of higher education has increased remarkably, mainly through gradual improvement of comprehensive basic education, wide geographical distribution of university education, and strong expansion of the polytechnic sector. One of the main arguments behind the expansion has been to include new groups in higher education and to reduce inequalities in gender, place of residence and social class.

As a consequence of this drive for expansion, Finland has among the highest levels of participation in higher education of any OECD member country. One-third of the population aged 25–64 has a tertiary qualification, and among younger adults (aged 25–34) the proportion is 40%, a level exceeded by only four OECD member countries. Approximately 7% of the population aged 15 or older is enrolled in tertiary education, the third-highest proportion in the OECD (MoE 2005).

Factors enabling equity in higher education

There are three primary factors enabling equity in Finnish higher education:

1. One important aspect of social equity is the system of comprehensive education. The OECD's Programme for International Student Assessment (PISA) consistently shows that Finnish 15-year-olds are the top performers among all participating nations on the combined mathematics-literacy test (Davies *et al.* 2006: 20). Finland is not only the best performing country, but belongs to the countries showing the least variation in performance both within and between schools. A closer analysis of the PISA results revealed that the strength of the relationship between student performance and socio-economic background was very low in Finland. These are all indications of a high degree of equality in basic education.

2. Finland's system of student support, among the more generous in OECD member nations, has the effect of removing credit constraints as an obstacle to tertiary study: those who want to study can do so without being deterred by their inability to finance their studies.

3. There are numerous opportunities offered to adults to undertake tertiary studies and the number of students enrolled in adult education is impressive. Open University education is free to everyone, regardless of age or educational background, and Open University instruction and courses are offered in almost all fields of study. There are also alternative modes of delivery for those adults prevented from taking part in campus-based learning, like distance learning and extension studies. Open Universities cannot award degrees, but the credits obtained are transferable and can be used as part of a degree if one enrols in a university later. More than 80 000 students participate in Open University education every year and courses are available at 200 localities throughout Finland. The Third Age University for older candidates, a special form of Open University, had 14 500 registered students in 2004. Every year Summer Universities (universities that only run courses during the summer) enrol nearly 70 000 students, including over 1 500 international students (Davies *et al.* 2006: 20).

The conditions for lifelong learning in Finland are in many respects favourable and might work in favour of equality in the long run. The differences between age groups in educational experience remain high in Finnish society, and adult education is used as a tool to equalise these differences. The different forms of open learning are well suited to meet the demand for lifelong learning and continuing education in the adult population. Their broad geographical dispersion and flexible organisation enables them to offer an extensive and varied range of teaching. In a sparsely populated country this is an important factor for promoting education equality. Evaluation studies of the Open University and Summer Universities have revealed that students can use them as a testing arena which can help them eventually enter university as regular students.

Finland has been very successful in improving geographic accessibility to higher education by regional expansion of the university system and the creation of polytechnics throughout the country. As stated earlier, 20 municipalities have a university (or campus) providing

Finland

degree studies and polytechnics are now established in 88 different localities. Open University studies can be pursued in a variety of units within the education network widely spread around the country.

Equity challenges

Notwithstanding these achievements, large inequalities in access to tertiary education by social origin still persist. Participation rates in university education among young students (aged 20–24) differ considerably according to the educational background of their parents. The relative chance of entering university education has remained at least ten times higher during the last decades for those coming from academic home backgrounds compared to students from less educated families. The expansion of the tertiary system appears to have narrowed the relative advantage of an academic home background to seven-fold (Davies *et al.* 2006: 21).

There is the potential for students who might benefit from tertiary study to be left behind, most especially in the transitions from lower-secondary to upper-secondary vocational education, and from upper secondary vocational education to tertiary education. Currently, the transition from vocational streams in secondary school to tertiary education is very low, and far behind the policy targets.

Higher education–labour market linkages

In many respects the higher education system has met the labour market challenges with great success. The decentralised system of university entry allows university departments to exercise independence with respect to entry qualifications, and to use this independence to select students whose skills and orientations are well matched to the demands of individual study programmes.

Universities have responded constructively to the Bologna degree structure,[2] and have used this opportunity to widen the range of study options available within universities, permitting students to choose between completing their studies with a Bachelor degree and continuing to the Masters level. In addition, there appears to be substantial opportunity for flexibility in university studies, in which students enrolled at one institution can, with permission, combine courses and programmes across separate university institutions. Employment and wage data reveal that graduates have opportunities to make productive use of their capacities, and are well rewarded for their schooling.

The polytechnics have widened the range of educational opportunities by offering a study option that provides earlier and less burdensome entry to study without the queuing characteristics of the university system; progression to degree completion that is comparatively swift; and a pedagogy and curriculum that are clearly focused on professional education, both at the Bachelor and Masters degree level.

A distinguishing feature is the central role assigned to labour market demand in the allocation of resources for higher education. State-funded study places are the central resource allocated by most ministries of education, and in Finland these are primarily allocated according to forecasts of labour market needs. These forecasts, adjusted to reflect policy targets for the government, then become the basis for a national Development Plan, a document that provides a five-year framework for education supply. The Development Plan provides the framework within which negotiations between the MoE and individual higher education institutions take place. Intake for each field of education is agreed between them, and contained in each institution's performance agreement with the Ministry. Seen in this light, Finland has a system of enrolment resource allocation that is not driven by student demand, but according to forecasts of labour market demand.

Higher education graduates fare significantly better in labour markets than do those without tertiary qualifications. If one compares all higher education graduates to those with secondary qualifications, rates of unemployment are lower and wages higher. Polytechnic graduates occupy a middle position between secondary and university graduates, both with respect to rates of unemployment and wages. And, among university graduates, the rate of unemployment diminishes and wages increase as the level of qualification increases (MoE 2005).

In many respects the system of tertiary education has connections to working life that are an international benchmark against which other systems might be judged. Those who complete a tertiary degree have high rates of employment, a significant wage premium, and private returns that compare favourably to those of graduates in other nations. This suggests that the relationship between the demand and supply of graduates is, on balance, holding up well.

Financing higher education

The role of the state in funding higher education is overwhelming. The following data, drawn from Davies *et al.* (2006) and MoE (2005), reveal the extent of the state's role in this regard:

- In 2002, public expenditure on higher education – both on institutions and subsidies to households – comprised 2.1% of GDP, the fourth-highest amongst 28 OECD countries for which data are available. This level of spending comprised 4.1% of all public expenditure, the fifth-highest level of any OECD country. Public expenditure on higher education grew 18% in real terms between 1999–2000 and 2004–2005, most of which was due to an expansion of enrolments (13%) and a modest share due to increased expenditures per student (4%).
- Finland is distinctive in its reliance on public financing for tertiary education. In 2002, 96.3% of all expenditures on higher education institutions were from public sources, and the remaining 3.7% from private sources.
- Along with its neighbours, Finland is one of a quartet of Nordic countries that spend at or above the OECD average of 1.36% of GDP on higher education, and for which 90% or more of all expenditure on education institutions comes from public sources.
- Although Finland spends a large share of public resources on higher education,

its annual expenditure on higher education institutions per student is 110% of the OECD average, only modestly above OECD average spending per student per year, at USD11 768, compared to the USD10 665 OECD average. This is due to the absence of significant private financing to complement public financing.

• Student support comprises a much larger share of all public spending on higher education than it does in the average OECD member country. About 18% of total spending on tertiary education is on student support, which is nearly double the OECD average.

Whilst institutional autonomy is respected, it is accepted that the MoE requires tools and instruments for the general steering of the system, and, by definition, some similarities in the instruments used to steer each sector, namely: performance agreements and the setting of target outcomes; core funding; national tasks and national programmes; performance-based funding; institutional reviews and monitoring of different types (mostly by the Ministry as an essential stage in the strategic planning cycle); and a statistical database.

There is general agreement that this range of instruments is well-conceived, policy-driven, and within an effective strategic planning cycle framework.

Recent changes in the Finnish system

A new University Act, effective from January 2010, brings about important changes to the way in which Finnish institutions are governed (Dobson 2009). In terms of the new Act, universities are required to appoint 40% of their board members from outside the institution. Three further reforms were proposed in the new legislation. First, there will be a major change to the way rectors are appointed. Like most of Europe, Finnish rectors have been elected by the professors, other staff and students. In future, the board will appoint the rector, who will be answerable to that board. The appointee will not need to be a professor of the university, as is currently required.

Second, universities' legal status will change: they will become independent legal entities rather than continuing to be 'accounting units' within the government bureaucracy. University staff will cease to be 'civil servants' and some have seen this change as an attack on academic freedom.

Finally, universities will have two-thirds ownership of companies that own university buildings and the government will be the minority shareholder. At present, universities rent buildings from a government-owned company, so the new legislation should provide universities with an asset they can use as leverage for borrowing from the capital markets.

There are important implications of the new legislation. First, it increases the role that outside stakeholders can play in the university. Second, it also increases university autonomy, particularly through giving them more responsibility for financing and staff policies. It is hoped that the reforms will create an environment in which universities can start to expand their funding base by acquiring funds from other sources, although this seems unlikely in the short term. Moreover, there is no intention at this stage to introduce tuition fees for domestic students.

Concluding observations and implications for African countries

It is evident that higher education in Finland influences economic development in the country in several ways. These include the following:

1. Higher education produces 'human capital' through its education and training function in the form of graduates in relatively high numbers and of high quality. These graduates contribute to economic development specifically and to overall development (including its social dimension) in a number of ways; for example, through their contribution to research, to education (as teachers) and to economic growth directly (e.g. engineers).

2. The higher education institutions place a strong emphasis on research and development and both the universities and the polytechnics in different ways play a critical role in the R&D function and in the innovation system as a whole.

3. Higher education is very closely linked to national and regional development policy. The higher education system of universities and polytechnics covers the whole country. Within this dual system, the universities are charged with academic research and the education which supports it, while polytechnics are charged with higher education geared to the world of work and research which serves education, the world of work and regional development.

4. The higher education system forms the basis for a regionally comprehensive innovation system which is regarded in the country as being critical for growth and development. In this system, universities and polytechnics are seen to be key components.

5. The higher education institutions play a key role with industry in enhancing regional development through their support and research role in such initiatives as the Centres of Expertise programme and the technology/science parks.

6. Recent research has shown the value of equity in stimulating growth and development. The commitment of the Finnish government to equity in general and of the higher education system in particular, must have been an important contributor to the high rates of economic growth experienced in Finland in recent decades.

7. The high success rates of graduates from the higher education system in the labour market in terms of both employment and earnings points both to the high levels of 'external efficiency' of the higher education system and to its clear role in promoting economic growth.

Finland

Drawing on the data and information presented in this chapter, some possible implications for African countries, based on the Finland experience, are outlined in the box below.

Box 3
The Finland experience: Possible implications for Africa

1. Linking economic and education planning: The Finnish system clearly illustrates the benefits of maintaining a close link between economic and education planning. This has been particularly true since policy decisions were taken to focus on the development of a knowledge economy. The link between higher education and national development has been a particularly close one. A feature of economic policy has been targeted intervention in the industrialisation process, with far-reaching implications for specific categories of outputs from the higher education system, such as engineering, science and teaching.

2. Building higher education on a sound foundation of high-quality, equitable schooling: The Finnish model shows how crucial high-quality schooling is for the development of a high-quality higher education system. An important aspect of social equity in Finland is the system of comprehensive education. The high quality of schooling provides a sound platform for a good quality, efficient higher education system.

3. A dual/binary higher education system can be effective in meeting national development goals: In Finland, the two higher education sub-sectors have fundamentally different roles. The polytechnics are seen as institutions which prepare their students for practical work, while the mission of the universities is more academic and has a theoretical and research orientation. However, the polytechnics also undertake research related to the world of work.

4. Polytechnics also play a broader, community-based education role: The polytechnics are involved in educational extension services including vocational education, adult education and vocational education research.

5. The state can play a dominant role in the development of an effective higher education system: The Finnish system demonstrates that the state, through its role in funding, can ensure the development of a higher education system that is appropriate to the country's needs.

6. Higher education can play an important role in regional development: Universities and polytechnics spread across the entire country work in collaboration with one another and with local government and business to ensure greater equity in regional development.

7. Cooperation and consensus is a key factor in policy-making and implementation: The Finnish system is characterised by a high degree of consensus-building and cooperation between stakeholders in the higher education system, including higher education institutions, government, public funding agencies and the private sector. This has been a key factor in stimulating efficiency and effectiveness in the distribution of resources and the development of appropriate education and research outcomes.

8. Appropriate institutional arrangements also help in the achievement of efficient and effective outcomes in higher education: The Finnish model illustrates clearly the value of appropriate institutional arrangements in a number of areas, whether it is with a view to developing consensus in strategic policy-making (e.g. Science and Technology Policy Council), ensuring efficient resource allocation (funding agencies), or designing a strong innovation system (private sector/government/ higher education institutions).

9. The higher education system must be able to meet the demands of the labour market: An outstanding feature of the Finnish higher education system is its great success in meeting the demands of the labour market. An important factor here has been the role of the state in providing disproportionate resources for scarce skills.

10. In summary, higher education is closely linked to economic and national development through its education and training role (the provider of human capital) and in its varied and wide-ranging roles in research and innovation.

Endnotes

1   Pers. comm., interview, Prof. Hölttä, September 2008.
2   The purpose of the Bologna Process (or Bologna Accords) was to create the European Higher Education Area by making academic standards and quality assurance standards more comparable and compatible throughout Europe.

CHAPTER 3

North Carolina

The higher education system

There are several key features of the North Carolina higher education system that are worth noting. These include the following:

1. Role of the state: There are at least two areas where the state plays a particularly prominent role, namely with respect to funding, and to engagement with institutions on the relationship between higher education and economic development:

   – The state provides substantial funding to higher education in the form of both block (unconditional) grants for teaching and research, and conditional grants for specific projects. At North Carolina State University (NCSU), for example, state funding comprises between 30% and 47% of the university's revenue. State funding is provided for, inter alia, instruction, agricultural extension, research activities and special infrastructure projects.
   – There is both strong general and specific support for higher education on the part of the state government and legislature, and a powerful sense of its importance for economic and social development.

2. There is a high level of productive engagement between higher education institutions and the private sector in addressing changing economic conditions. The following examples serve to illustrate the nature of this relationship:

   – During the last 15–20 years, the nature of the private economic sector has changed towards high value-adding, highly-skilled sub-sectors such as biotechnology, pharmaceuticals and biomanufacturing. There has been a corresponding shift in the higher education sector to meet the demand for these skills.
   – The Golden Leaf Fund, a private sector initiative, established a USD60 million grant to better link graduates to the work environment.
   – The North Carolina higher education system has a long history of responsiveness to the labour market and private sector. It has the ability to shift and change course quickly.

3. There are good linkages between universities and other post-secondary institutions (community colleges), particularly with respect to a clear division of roles, as well as articulation.

4. Community colleges address two basic challenges: that of workforce (skills) development, and of providing access to those unable to attend universities in the first instance.

5. There is considerable university specialisation (differentiation) in the public system. For example, in the Research Triangle area, the two major public institutions – the University of North Carolina (UNC) at Chapel Hill and the NCSU – rarely duplicate high-cost faculties such as medicine and engineering. The state university system is of varying quality but the large institutions are of very high quality. In a recent survey, UNC (Chapel Hill) was placed first among 120 national universities and colleges in terms of 'value for money' in public higher education institutions with respect to quality and cost, with NCSU placed 13th (Clark 2008).

6. Institutional arrangements and networks: The public university system is much more unified than the system in almost any other American state, with all 16 institutions falling under one University of North Carolina General Administration (UNCGA). The president of the UNCGA is often a politically astute person with private-sector experience and a serious commitment to higher education. For example, the 2007–2008 president was once a successful banker and also served as Chief of Staff in the Clinton White House.

On budgetary matters, the UNGCA negotiates with the governor and the legislature on behalf of all 16 institutions, which are not supposed to negotiate independently. This arrangement has been very beneficial to the UNC system: the state of North Carolina puts more money into higher education per capita than any other state that is capable of similar economies of scale. Notwithstanding this level of centralisation in dealing with the state of North Carolina, the individual institutions run their affairs completely independently within the bounds of some constraints set by the UNGCA.

The funding mechanisms/arrangements vary from specific contracts (which are applied through sales and services agreements, and memoranda of understanding – a legal understanding between a unit in the North Carolina state higher education system and a unit in the state government), to legislative special funding, and consortial arrangements across either a group of institutions and/or institutions and non-profit agencies.

The different colleges and universities handle research, research grants and their relationships with the private sector in their own ways (although the UNGCA can place some reasonable and not very restrictive constraints on them). Committees are not as important as they are, for example, in South Africa, the United Kingdom or Australia. Funds that come from the private sector do not have to be vetted and approved by the administration. At NCSU, for example, there are vice-chancellors for research; extension, engagement and economic development; and university advancement. These individuals, who report to the chief executive officer or chancellor, are supposed to champion and facilitate developments in their fields. They have executive responsibility and are not hidebound by committees. There are some committees, for example, to consider research leave applications, but they tend to be small working groups. The system thus attempts to minimise the danger of 'bureaucratic blockages' to the efficient running of the institution. At the academic management level, moreover, there are numerous faculty committees and sub-committees.

The North Carolina Community College System

The mission of the North Carolina Community College System (NCCCS) is to open the door to high-quality, accessible educational opportunities that minimise barriers to post-secondary education; maximise student success; develop a globally and multi-culturally competent workforce; and improve the lives and well-being of individuals.

There are two components to the NCCCS, namely continuing education (workforce development) and an associate degree,[1] with graduates emerging with a two-year community college degree.

The NCCCS is North Carolina's primary agency for the delivery of job training, literacy and adult education. The system served more than 800 000 students through its 58 institutions in the 2005–2006 academic year. The NCCCS is located in 90 counties across the state with 156 additional campuses or off-campus centres, in addition to the 58 main campuses with service areas of one or more counties. On the degree side, the state legislature provides funding on the basis of full-time equivalents, and separate funding for capital equipment and capacity-building for the training of specific categories of human resources (e.g. nursing instructors). Each college in the system is autonomous, with its own board, and is funded centrally. The private sector funds the continuing education of the workforce through a number of short, non-credit courses. A small business centre in each college is funded by the legislature.

There is also a bio-technology network – a joint initiative between community colleges and the NCSU. According to a senior official in the NCCCS, there is a very close relationship with the Department of Commerce and community colleges.[2]

The sense of partnership (between community colleges and the state, between community colleges and regional universities, and between community colleges and the state government) is overwhelming and undoubtedly an important factor in the success of the NCCCS.

The average age of community-college students is 34 and more than two-thirds of these work while attending college. Community colleges train more nurses, emergency medical technicians, paid and volunteer fire-fighters, and local enforcement personnel than any other education agency in the state. More than 95% of community college students are in-state residents who remain and work in the state after completion, thereby contributing to the state's economy.

The NCCCS provides an opportunity for high-school students to take college courses not otherwise available, to enhance their motivation and achievement, and to encourage them

North Carolina

to pursue lifelong education and training goals. In 2005–2006, more than 21 000 high-school students took college classes tuition-free.

The NCCCS provided basic education and literacy resources to more than 135 000 adults in 2005–2006. These are the skills needed to prepare adults to seek employment and to give them the ability to become full partners in the educational development of their children.

Community college students have convenient access to quality education and training resources through online instruction, videoconferencing, telecourse/teleweb, hybrid courses, and web supplements for traditional classroom courses.

Economic and workforce development programmes
North Carolina has been extremely innovative in the training of the skilled workforce. Through the community colleges, a system was created for the training of the workforce. This training is aimed at three categories of individuals: new entrants into the workforce, entrepreneurs, and those unemployed through social programmes.

Systematic focus, flexibility in meeting new demands for economic development, and workforce development continue to be a hallmark of the support provided by the NCCCS. The NCCCS is committed to the purpose of creating a workforce and stimulating economic growth and development as a full partner in the process in each geographic region of the state.

The types of programmes offered include the following:

- The New and Expanding Industry Training Program supports the expansion of existing businesses and the attraction of new industry enterprise to North Carolina.
- The Focused Industrialised Training Program responded to a variety of training needs with a significant number of the state's business or industrial firms. The programme provided targeted opportunities for the incumbent workforce to be re-trained to meet the demands of new technologies or procedures required for existing companies to be more competitive and productive.
- The Customized Industrialised Training Program offered programmes and training services as new options for assisting business and industry to remain productive, profitable and within the state. The programme provided the flexibility to meet the re-training needs for existing business organisation in North Carolina's communities.
- The Workforce Continuing Education Program provides significant services to those who seek additional skills for a changing economy or to those citizens displaced who could take advantage of training resources to re-train for new jobs.
- The Small Business Center Network attempts to enhance and expand its outreach to both aspiring entrepreneurs and existing small-business owners throughout North Carolina in the rural and metropolitan areas.
- The Human Resources Development Program seeks to respond to the changing needs and demographics of individuals seeking workforce development training.

The programme provides counselling and training assistance to the unemployed and under-employed citizens of North Carolina to improve their ability to get a job or continue their education to enhance their preparation for greater employment opportunities.

- The BioNetwork Program has three main goal areas – workforce development, economic development, and infrastructure development – and identifies key goals in each area. The goals are focused on growing BioNetwork's capabilities and ensuring a high level of quality of the training and education provided by the organisation.

In sum, the community colleges undertake workforce development for new companies, expanding companies, automating industries and small business, as well as workforce continuing education.

The NCCCS is interesting, from a developing country perspective, for a number of reasons, including the following:

- It offers unlimited opportunities for students who are unable to go to university to pursue post-secondary education and attain an associate degree.
- Those who qualify from the community college with an associate degree can then go on to university.
- Continuing education through workforce development and other adult education programmes is possible throughout one's life.
- The workforce development programmes to enhance skills provide wide choice and are tuned to the wide-ranging needs of a growing economy.
- The success of the NCCCS is due in no small measure to the strong and productive relationships that have developed with universities, private sector and government with respect both to funding and to identifying educational and training opportunities to enhance economic development.

University–industry linkages: The case of NCSU

The NCSU[3] provides an excellent case study of a higher education institution that has developed close, productive linkages with the private sector to promote economic development.

Grounded in the land-grant mission to 'transform lives and improve the human condition through innovation and discovery' (NCSU 2008), NCSU has built a strong tradition of partnerships with community, business and government. For this, the Carnegie Foundation recently designated the university as an 'engaged university' – engaging students in the curricula, and both students and faculty in community outreach.

NCSU has also demonstrated considerable creativity and entrepreneurship in its 552 United States patents and 533 active license agreements with industry to commercialise academic research. In the past 25 years, NCSU, operating as a knowledge base for the state, has launched 63 companies, creating more than 13 000 jobs and generating more than USD200 million in follow-on venture capital investments, most of this new capital going into the state.

North Carolina

In 2007–2008, NCSU launched seven companies, received 49 patents, and executed 81 industry agreements, formalising partnerships between the university and corporate partners and generating USD3.6 million in royalties from commercialised products. In the fiscal year of 2006, Scientist magazine ranked NCSU third in the nation for overall patent power (NCSU 2008).

The following sections describe a number of university–industry linkages that have enhanced economic growth and promoted economic development in the region.

Generating jobs and investment locally, regionally and statewide with unique strategies

Between 2006 and 2008, NCSU and Wake County (the local government) Economic Development worked together to transform hi-tech research into well-paying jobs. The Economic Development Partnership taps into the resources of NCSU and researchers to glean leads about companies, matching the companies' needs to the manufacturing, research and development capabilities of the state and the 13-county Research Triangle region. The partners then develop a customised approach to attract industry-specific companies to the area. It is a long-term cycle of identifying companies, creatively partnering them with the university, creating new products, and encouraging them not to manufacture those products elsewhere. Forbes magazine, in its 2007 annual survey of the top 100 cities in the United States, ranked the Raleigh-Cary area (in which NCSU is located) the number one metropolitan area for jobs in the country (NCSU 2008).

Targeting the non-woven textiles industry

The first targeted companies in North Carolina were the non-woven textiles companies. Since the partnership between this industry and NCSU was initiated in 2004, ten companies have moved operations to North Carolina and invested more than USD240 million in the state. Today North Carolina has the largest concentration of non-woven companies in the nation.

Inside NCSU's Non-woven Cooperative Research Center (NCRC) – home to the most comprehensive non-woven textiles laboratory in the world – heavy machines roll out 300m of material per minute. This is more than 1 000 times faster than the looms inside traditional textile mills. A fabric line inside NCRC turns out more material in one hour than 500 looms weave in four hours. NCRC is thus a resource for product development, research, and training for non-woven companies. Just as its engines turn out staggering volumes of fabric, the centre has proved to be an engine for continuing growth. With this success and nearly 80 member companies worldwide, the NCRC is the largest industry-sponsored, university-based consortium in the United States.

According to the Executive Director of Wake County Economic Development, Ken Atkins, the continuing collaborative successes of the Economic Development Partnership have paved the way for targeting and attracting other industry sectors, including medical devices, bio-manufacturing and bio-medical research.

Extending NCSU's resources and reach

At NCSU, the concept of the 'engaged university' extends across the state to individual communities. The College of Agriculture and Life Sciences has extension offices in each of North Carolina's 100 counties and on the Cherokee reservation; the Industrial Extension service in 21 locations; and the Small Business Technology and Development Center (SBTDC) at 16 UNC campuses. The College of Design staff, for example, study traffic and develop planning strategies for communities on the Outer Banks, and the College of Agriculture and Life Sciences is opening a food product incubator in Orange County.

Bringing more research opportunities in next-generation electronics

NCSU remains on the forefront of other emerging industries as well. The two-year-old Center for Efficient, Secure and Reliable Computing (CESR) – one of only a handful of university research centres focused on embedded systems – is creating the next generation of electronics: Red Hat, a world leader in opensource software with headquarters on Centennial Campus, has partnered with CESR to bring more research opportunities and jobs to North Carolina. Cell-phone manufacturer Qualcomm and semiconductor manufacturer Renesas Technology have established design operations in North Carolina – in part for the opportunity to work with CESR researchers.

Collaborating on Centennial Campus to solve contemporary problems

The leaders at NCSU believe that the establishment of Centennial Campus for private sector-university collaboration adds to the university's national visibility. This environmentally sensitive, mixed-use academic village responds to the professional, educational and recreational needs of the university's faculty, staff and student body, as well as those of corporate and government affiliates whose presence on Centennial Campus adds to its vigour and effectiveness. Home to NCRC and a national model for partnerships among business, government and the university, more than 130 companies, government agencies, and NCSU research and academic units have resided on Centennial Campus. Twenty-three start-up companies are located in the North Carolina State Technology Incubator and, during 2007–2008, 12 new partners joined the campus while the number of major partners continues to expand.

The American Home Project on Centennial Campus has the vision to be the premier research, education and extension facility for housing in the country. With five demonstration homes and an academic building, it is an initiative for discovery and learning to advance and demonstrate innovation in the industry.

There is a clear belief here that entrepreneurship is critical to the state and country's economic health and growth in the 21st century. In this regard, NCSU appears to be committed to entrepreneurial education in a number of ways; for example, through developing an experiential learning activity for undergraduates, and an introduction to social entrepreneurship. Increasingly, the university environment is nurturing entrepreneurs for the private, non-profit and public sectors. Through its Entrepreneurship Education Initiative in the College of Management and Engineering Entrepreneurs Program, students go from creative idea or innovation to business planning and start-up. And, in Management, Design, Engineering, Textiles and other colleges, a variety of courses focus on design of new products and discovery of new markets, technology transfer and commercialising new innovations. With its state-wide entrepreneurship and cluster-based economic development agenda, NCSU supports micro-enterprises with high-growth potential, with a focus on rural areas and less-developed local governments.

Expanding impact on small- and medium-sized enterprises in high growth sectors

The SBTDC is well-recognised within the economic development and business communities as an important educational and technical assistance resource for entrepreneurs; the expansion of existing businesses; and technology development and commercialisation. Acknowledged for its high-quality, in-depth business counselling and management education services to small- and medium-sized businesses, its professional staff serves nearly 13 000 individuals. The SBTDC plans to strengthen levels of outreach and services to less-developed local governments in each of its regions, and to expand the capacity of the Cooperative Extension Service by training and support through the SBTDC offices.

Supporting advanced medical care

The economic development partnership between Wake County Economic Development and NCSU is expanding its efforts beyond the College of Textiles to the College of Veterinary Medicine. Next up are bio-technology partnerships developed in collaboration with the College of Veterinary Medicine – home to the Centennial Biomedical Campus, an extension of the Centennial Campus concept that will include 1.6 million square feet of building space dedicated to biomedical applications for animals and humans. At the Center for Comparative Medicine and Translational Research, interactions between different laboratories as well as interactions with private groups enhance collaborative, translational interdisciplinary approaches for the comparative study of animal/human diseases. Supporting these efforts, the Biomedical Textiles and Device Innovation Consortium will focus on coalescing multi-college resources such as those from the colleges of Engineering, Management, Design and Textiles to assist new product development, testing and commercialisation efforts within the regional medical device, and advanced medical care industry clusters.

In summary, with respect to university-industry linkages and their role in promoting economic development, three features stand out in the relationship between higher education (as exemplified by NCSU), on the one hand, and the private sector and government, on the other. These include the following:

- Innovation: A culture of innovation has been fostered that encourages and rewards intellectual leadership on the part of both staff and students through, inter alia, pioneering new methods of instruction and a highly relevant curricula in a multi-disciplinary academic approach.
- Research: The institution is research-focused and deeply engaged in knowledge discovery and application driven by its disciplines.
- Partnerships: There are active and unique partnerships with business, government, community, other universities and schools. By leveraging these partnerships, along with its own Centennial Campus and proximity to and association with the world-famous Research Triangle Park, the university has succeeded in creating a dynamic and rewarding learning environment.

Economic development has essentially been modelled through the following:

- Utilising university resources through partnerships to foster economic development
- Collaborative partnerships
- Effective utilisation of university resources – staff and students, expertise and facilities
- Communities, industries and government, and
- Community impacts.

Identifying future challenges in higher education: The UNC Tomorrow Commission

The North Carolina higher education system recently established a multi-stakeholder commission called the UNC Tomorrow Commission to investigate and report on the challenges facing higher education and the state. The findings of the commission are relevant to developing countries to the extent that the challenges identified are precisely those facing this group of countries as well. It is therefore worth providing some detail on both the findings and recommendations, given the high degree of commonality across both industrialised and developing countries with respect to challenges facing higher education policy-makers and implementers. However, it has to be borne in mind that while the nature of the challenges might be similar, they differ substantially in the degree to which they occur in both sets of countries (that is, industrialised and developing). Moreover, the industrialised countries (and even regions within such countries, such as North Carolina) have substantially more resources at their disposal to address these challenges.

The purpose of the UNC Tomorrow Commission was to determine how the UNC could respond more directly and proactively to 21st-century challenges facing North Carolina through the fulfilment of its three-pronged mission of teaching, research and scholarship, and public service. The outcomes of this initiative were supposed to guide and shape current and future priorities, resource allocations, existing and future programmes, and strategic plans and missions of the UNC, its 17 constituent institutions and its affiliated entities. The purpose was to ensure that UNC not only becomes more proactive and responsive to the needs of the state, but remains so in the years to come, as the people of North Carolina continue to confront the many challenges of the rapidly changing, knowledge-based global economy and environment of the 21st century.

The UNC Tomorrow Commission was guided by the UNC Board of Governors' chairperson, the UNC president and the UNC Tomorrow Commission – a 28-member group including business, education, government and non-profit leaders from across the state. The commission was charged with the responsibility of learning what the people of North Carolina needed from their university and making relevant recommendations to the UNC Board of Governors.

To become more responsive to the needs and challenges of the state, UNC first had to identify what those needs and challenges were. This was accomplished through visits to all UNC campuses; 11 community listening forums across the state, attended by approximately

North Carolina

2 700 members of the public; 11 faculty forums involving all 17 UNC campuses, attended by almost 1 000 students and staff; an online survey to which 6 700 people responded; and a blog hosted on the UNC Tomorrow website. Through these efforts, UNC Tomorrow listened to what the people of North Carolina, the faculty and the students told them about what they needed from their public university to help address the significant challenges facing their own future and that of their communities, regions and the state as a whole.

Major findings of the UNC Tomorrow Commission

This section describes some of the findings of the Tomorrow Commission (UNC 2007). Its detailed recommendations and suggested strategies are described in Appendix 2.

Box 4
Major findings of the UNC Tomorrow Commission

1. Global readiness
2. Access to higher education
3. Improving public education
4. Economic transformation
5. Health
6. Environment
7. Outreach and engagement

Global readiness

The major finding with regard to 'global readiness' was that UNC should educate its students to be personally and professionally successful in the 21st century and, to do so, should enhance the global competitiveness of its institutions and their graduates. In this regard, UNC should prepare its students for successful professional and personal lives, equipping them with the tools they will need to adapt to the ever-changing world. UNC programmes, especially research programmes, should be globally competitive to ensure that they are globally relevant and significant. Furthermore, UNC should promote increased partnerships between its own campuses and international universities and enhance the global awareness of its faculty and students.

Shortage of college skills in the workforce – According to the Tomorrow Commission Report, if North Carolina is to succeed in the global economic and knowledge race, forecasts indicate that more and better education will have to be provided to more people. It is estimated that by 2020 the shortage of workers with college-level skills in the United States will increase to more than 14 million (UNC 2007). To meet the demands for more educated workers in the state, the North Carolina Commission on Workforce Development estimated that the state will have to produce 15 000 more workers annually with at least a Bachelors degree, and 19 000 more workers with a two-year degree, than it is currently. While about 33% of North Carolina's college-age students are enrolled in college, this rate is only 69% of that in South Korea, and is also lower than the rates in Greece, Finland, Ireland and Poland. Moreover, these graduates must possess the 'hard skills' that are relevant to the global economy and to dynamic business needs, such as expertise in science, mathematics and technology. However, in the United States, only about 16% of undergraduate degrees are awarded in the science, technology, engineering and mathematics fields, while in China more than 50% of undergraduate degrees are in these fields.

Shortage of 'soft skills' – Importantly, the Commission also noted that today's college students need to develop 'soft skills' – capabilities including the ability to think critically, reason analytically, solve problems, communicate clearly both orally and in writing, work in teams, and be comfortable within a diverse workforce. These skills, which are critical to lifelong learning and professional growth, have become a necessity as economic sectors, occupations and job characteristics continue to change more rapidly today than in the past. In many instances, it is proficiency with the soft skills, along with the ability to think innovatively and creatively, that will carry students from one job or career to another. The technical skills required of students are changing so rapidly that the university is preparing students today to work in jobs that do not yet exist, with technologies that are still unknown. What will not change, however, is the need for these critical soft skills.

Access to higher education

The major finding here was that UNC should increase access to higher education for all North Carolinians, particularly for under-served regions, under-represented populations and non-traditional students.

UNC should increase access to its educational programmes – including academic courses, degree programmes at all levels, and certificate programmes – for traditional students, non-traditional students and lifelong learners. UNC should continue ongoing efforts with the NCCCS to strengthen and streamline articulation between the two systems so as to develop a more seamless relationship. Moreover, UNC should be a model for accommodating the needs of persons with disabilities, including students, faculty, staff and the general public. UNC should also maintain affordability and increase financial aid options. UNC should increase the educational attainment of all under-represented populations, especially African-American male and Hispanic students. Finally, UNC should help to ensure that all students are better prepared to enter, and succeed academically in, college.

Increasing access to higher education was seen as critical to North Carolina's future. As the state continues to transform socially and economically in the 21st-century knowledge-based global environment, higher education attainment becomes increasingly important for the population.

There are, however, regions of North Carolina and certain population groups that face significant obstacles to successfully attaining post-secondary education, including low- and moderate-income students, African-American males, and the state's rapidly growing Hispanic student population. Moreover, the dynamic changes in today's workforce create an increased demand for higher education among working adults, non-traditional students and lifelong learners.

Given the increasing importance of higher education to economic competitiveness in today's knowledge-based global economy, limiting access to affordable higher education for the state's under-served groups raises serious concerns about the state's ability to

North Carolina

remain competitive in the years ahead. Moreover, the current obstacles, both educational and financial, that such students face in pursuing higher education, threaten to relegate them to permanent underclass status, which has serious social and fiscal implications, including increased social services and criminal justice costs.

Improving public education

The major finding here was that UNC should be more actively involved in solving North Carolina's public education challenges. In this regard, UNC should improve the quantity, quality and geographic distribution of public school teachers. UNC should help address the shortage of science and mathematics teachers, especially in rural areas. UNC should also strengthen efforts, in cooperation with the North Carolina State Board of Community Colleges and the Community College System, the North Carolina State Board of Education, and the North Carolina Department of Public Instruction, to enhance the teaching skills of public-school faculty and the leadership skills of public-school administrators. UNC should leverage its expertise and increase collaborations with the State Board of Education and the Department of Public Instruction to help lower the state's dropout rate and improve academic achievement in all public schools in North Carolina, especially those that are high-priority and low-performing. UNC should strengthen partnerships with the State Board of Education, the North Carolina Department of Public Instruction, the North Carolina Community College System, and the state's Independent Colleges and Universities to develop a seamless educational continuum from pre-primary through to higher education.

Economic transformation

The major finding here is that UNC should be more actively engaged in enhancing the economic transformation and community development of North Carolina's regions and the state as a whole.

Here it was imperative that UNC increase its capacity and commitment to respond to and lead economic transformation and community development. UNC should focus specific effort on meeting the needs of rural and under-served areas of the state. UNC should also seek to align appropriate campus programmes with the strategic economic plans (including sector and cluster plans) of their regions and the state, recognising the unique differences and challenges of the state's economic and geographic regions.

It was recognised that North Carolina is in the midst of a major economic transformation. The traditional industries that built the state in the 20th century – tobacco, textiles and furniture – were now downsizing in the face of globalisation, international competition and changing consumer preferences. Fortunately, new industries – including technology, pharmaceuticals and finance – have developed to take their place, but the transition has not been smooth. While thousands of citizens have seen their lives improve in the hi-tech global marketplace of the 21st century, many others have been left behind. The distinguishing feature between the two populations is at the core of UNC's mission: education.

Education in the new economy has divided North Carolina in two ways. First, it has divided the workers. Workers with higher levels of educational attainment have in large part done well in today's economy – a striking similarity with the South African economy.

The modern economy's focus on subject-matter knowledge, as well as problem-solving and interpersonal skills, has meant workers with these traits have succeeded and moved up the economic ladder. In contrast, workers with modest levels of educational attainment have faced a much different job market. They have seen low-skill, moderate-income jobs, easily found in previous decades, migrate increasingly to foreign countries where labour costs are lower. This has left modestly educated workers qualified for an ample number of service-sector jobs, but these jobs generally pay less.

The diverse paths of more-educated and less-educated workers in North Carolina are clearly seen in the statistics. During the 2000s, only college-educated workers experienced wage increases that exceeded inflation. Workers with less than a college education saw their inflation-adjusted wages fall. Furthermore, the fastest expanding jobs have been those at the high and low ends of the pay scale. Jobs with moderate rates of pay have been growing at the slowest pace. This phenomenon has been termed the 'hollowing-out' of the job market, or the 'disappearing middle'.

Geographic considerations – The new North Carolina economy has also divided the state geographically. Economic growth and improvements in living standards have been most rapid in metropolitan counties and have been slower or stagnant in many rural and small-town counties. Again, the determining factor seems to be education. Counties with higher levels of educational attainment among their workers – usually metro counties – have been more successful in creating and attracting the new industries of the 21st century and enhancing job opportunities.

These 21st-century economic trends show no signs of abating and might even accelerate. The rest of the world also recognises the benefits of education, 'soft skills', analytical reasoning and problem-solving. Traditional trading partners in Europe and the Western Hemisphere, in addition to new trading partners in Asia, are all putting increased focus on education and skills development. The competition for the best jobs and the best pay will only get stiffer, moving increasingly from low-skill, low-wage jobs to higher-skill, higher-wage jobs.

All of these factors suggest that UNC's mission will play a vital role on several levels in the decades ahead. First and foremost, UNC should continue to educate and equip North Carolinians with the talents and skills necessary to be successful in today's highly competitive, internationally-linked world. UNC should be prepared to do this for a more diverse student body, perhaps in ways very different than in the past. UNC also should do more to apply its resources and knowledge base to the economic issues facing specific geographic regions in the state. Finally, UNC should serve as an 'interpreter of change' – understanding and anticipating broad trends in the economy and workforce, and communicating the meaning and implications of those trends to both private and public sector decision-makers.

Health

The major finding here was that UNC should lead in improving the health and wellness of all people and communities in the state through, inter alia, educating more health professionals.

North Carolina

Environment

The major finding here was that UNC should assume a leadership role in addressing the state's energy and environmental challenges. UNC should embrace environmental sustainability as a core value among its institutions. It should leverage its existing research expertise to address critical environmental and energy issues. UNC should increase community awareness of environmental and sustainability issues. The point made here was that the future of the North Carolina economy, the quality of its environment and how energy is used are intricately and inseparably intertwined.

Outreach and engagement

The major finding here was that UNC should become more directly engaged with and connected to the people of North Carolina, its regions and the state as a whole. In this regard, UNC should apply, translate and communicate research and scholarship to broader audiences. UNC should also develop a strategic plan for scholarly public service on each campus that is detailed and specific in definition and scope. UNC should create a mechanism for applying research and scholarship to addressing significant regional and state-wide issues. It should also communicate its resources and expertise to wider audiences.

In summary, the UNC Tomorrow Commission acknowledges the importance of higher education, first, for economic development narrowly (note its recommendations on global readiness and economic transformation), and, second, for sustainable development more broadly (note its concern for health and environmental issues, for example). In other words, it is recognised that the challenges of higher education go beyond 'pure education issues' to those relating both to globalisation and the local environment.

Concluding observations and implications for African countries

Before concluding with some possible implications of the North Carolina experience for African policy-makers, an important caveat is needed. This case study looked at the higher education system of a state within the most industrialised country and one of the richest in the world. The financial, human and other resources available to this system far exceed what is available to the average African country, indeed to the continent as a whole. Income per capita in North Carolina is similarly many times in excess of the average for Africa, as well as for the richest African countries. The lessons that can be drawn from such a case study have to be viewed in this rich-country, advanced-region context.

However, the schooling system in North Carolina faces many developing country-type challenges, especially with regard to access and quality. Participation in higher education is relatively low compared to countries such as Finland and South Korea, and highly inequitable in terms of race, class and region.

Nevertheless, there are several features of the North Carolina higher education system that are important with respect to its impact on development. First, the state plays an important role in funding, and in promoting engagement between higher education institutions and the private sector. Second, there is a high level of productive engagement between higher education institutions and the private sector, particularly in response to changing economic conditions. Third, there are very good linkages between universities and other post-secondary institutions (such as community colleges), particularly with regard to ensuring a clear division of roles and articulation. Fourth, the community colleges address two basic challenges: that of workforce/skills development, and providing access to those unable to attend universities in the first instance. Fifth, the North Carolina universities, particularly the two leading institutions, have developed productive linkages with the private sector to enhance economic development through research and development and cultivating a culture of innovation. Sixth, there is increasing recognition that universities can play a greater role in improving the quantity, quality and distribution of teachers; helping to address the shortage of science and mathematics teachers; and strengthening efforts to help schools to reduce drop out and repetition rates. In other words, there is an important role for public universities in helping to raise the quality of school education, a key factor for the success of higher education.

Drawing on the data and information presented in this chapter, some possible implications for African countries, based on the North Carolina experience, are outlined in the box below.

Box 5
The North Carolina experience: Possible implications for Africa

1. Clarifying the role of higher education in development: Higher education is recognised as important for economic and broader social and environmental development (i.e. sustainable development). This is particularly so in a rapidly globalising world where patterns of economic development are no longer homogenous, as in the 19th and early 20th centuries.

2. The success of higher education is critically dependent on improving public school education. This implies increasing access and equity, and improving the quality and efficiency of education at all levels.

3. The post-secondary sector, including universities and community colleges (or their equivalent), must be appropriately differentiated to cater to the differing needs of the population and the economy.

4. The higher education sector should be sufficiently flexible to respond to changing labour market conditions.

5. Effective relationships need to be developed between the higher education system, on the one hand, and government, private business sector and civil society broadly, on the other, to promote economic, social and environmental development.

North Carolina

Endnotes

1 An associate degree is awarded by community colleges – as opposed to 'full' degrees awarded by universities. An associate degree holder can go on to university and attain a full degree.

2 Pers. comm., Interview, Ms Willa Dickens, Economic Workforce Development, North Carolina Community College System, March 2008

3 www.ncsu.edu; www.ncsu.edu/extension

CHAPTER 4

South Korea

South Korean economic development

South Korea has experienced rapid and sustained economic growth since the 1960s when South Korea's gross domestic product (GDP) per capita was comparable to levels in the poorer countries of Africa (in 1960 it was USD1 110 compared to USD430 for sub-Saharan Africa) (Suh & Chen 2007: 5). Forty-five years after the full-scale, government-led industrialisation drive that started in the early 1960s, South Korea's GDP per capita had increased more than twelve-fold to more than USD13 000 in 2005. Moreover, its GDP per capita increased from USD67 in 1953 to USD20 050 in 2007 (Suh & Chen 2007: 6).

As Table 4 below shows, in 1960 South Korea's GDP per capita was twice that of sub-Saharan Africa's, but in 2005 it was almost 24 times as much, reflecting the divergence of development in South Korea and sub-Saharan Africa respectively.

Table 4
Comparative GDP per capita: South Korea, sub-Saharan Africa, OECD (USD)

Year	South Korea	Sub-Saharan Africa	OECD
1960	1 110	430	9 137
1980	3 221	583	17 710
2005	13 210	560	29 376

Source: Grubb *et al.* (2006); Suh and Chen (2007)

The economic policies that have underpinned this growth have emphasised the development of a vigorous, export-orientated manufacturing industry, with a progressive shift towards high technology. South Korea remains more dependent upon manufacturing than nearly all Organisation for Economic Cooperation and Development (OECD) countries. In 2003, manufacturing accounted for 26% of gross value-added, a figure exceeded only by Ireland with 31%. One-third (35%) of the civilian labour force is employed in manufacturing, one of the highest levels in the OECD, and only two-thirds (64%) in the service sector, one of the lowest (Grubb *et al.* 2006).

Current economic policy favours a continued strong manufacturing sector with a higher technological base, rather than a significant shift towards the service sector. There has however been significant expansion of knowledge-based industries, both in manufacturing and in the service sector in recent years. In 2000, high- and medium-technology and knowledge-intensive manufacturing represented a higher proportion of total gross value-added in South Korea (close to 15%) than in any OECD country other than Ireland (Grubb *et al.* 2006).

South Korean development strategy

Educational investment has undoubtedly played a significant role in South Korea's rapid and sustained economic growth. Development strategies have focused on achieving sustained productivity growth by consistently increasing the value-added of output. To achieve this, a highly educated labour force was necessary. In the 1960s, South Korea embarked on the promotion of both export and import-substitution industries, starting with subsistence agriculture (rice) and labour-intensive, light manufacturing sectors (textiles and bicycles). Considerable capital accumulation and investment in primary education during this period allowed a gradual shift up the value-added chain toward more sophisticated commodities. Key to this shift was also the use of technologies obtained through foreign licensing and adapted for domestic production.

In the mid-1970s, the government's use of a well-targeted industrial policy resulted in a major shift to the development of heavy industries (e.g., chemicals and shipbuilding). Along with industrial targeting, policies were enacted to further improve technological capabilities, together with improving access to and quality of technical and vocational training.

In the 1980s, South Korea undertook efforts to ensure a market-conducive environment by deregulating various sectors and liberalising trade. Concurrently, it expanded higher education while investing in indigenous research and development through the establishment of the National Research and Development Program.

South Korea continued to pursue high value-added manufacturing in the 1990s by promoting indigenous high-technology innovation. Domestic wage hikes and the appreciation of the currency had resulted in chronic current account deficits, which sparked a series of reforms, including the reform of the financial market. Together with the setting up of a modern and accessible information infrastructure, there was continued expansion of research and development capabilities in South Korean industries, which drew on the skilled labour force that had resulted from the government's expansion of the higher education system.

In the aftermath of the financial crisis in the mid-1990s, policy efforts were made to transform the South Korean economy into a knowledge-based one in which innovation could thrive, enhancing overall productivity and thereby sustaining economic growth.

Many factors have enabled South Korea's rapid change. Key amongst these were the building of an information infrastructure and harnessing the potential of science and technology.

Building an information infrastructure

South Korea's successful movement toward an information society is the result of concerted effort by government and industry. The government has tried to lay down the information infrastructure, whereas industry, benefiting from the government's initiative, has consistently tried to capitalise on the information infrastructure and existing technologies. Since the mid-1990s, South Korea has pushed for a strong national and social information infrastructure. As a result, it now has one of the world's top broadband internet infrastructures. At the end of 2000, 144 major cities and regions were connected by high-speed broadband networks through fibre-optic cables. As of June 2004, 66% of the population had access to the internet (Suh & Chen 2007: 13).

However, despite the widespread use of information technology, South Korea has yet to translate the rapid spread of its information infrastructure into qualitative results, such as increased industrial competitiveness and entrepreneurial innovation.

Harnessing the potential of science and technology
Although South Korea, as a late-industrialising country, has depended heavily on foreign technologies, it has also made an effort to accumulate technological capabilities. At the initial launch of its economy-wide development plan, South Korea was poorly endowed with factors necessary for industrialisation, except for a plentiful labour force. Furthermore, the technological competence of South Korean firms was far below world standards. Consequently, it was inevitable or natural that it would look toward foreign sources for technologies. After the industrialisation process was launched in 1962, there was remarkable growth in imports of foreign technologies.

The process of technological capability in South Korea is characterised as a dynamic process involving the interplay between imported technologies and indigenous research and development (R&D) efforts. However, as is described later, the R&D efforts are largely the consequence of initiatives by public research institutes rather than the universities. Furthermore, the configuration of South Korea's innovation system has largely been shaped by overall economic development strategies.

Education and economic development

Education has been a key factor in South Korea's rapid economic growth over the past four decades. Since the 1960s, the government-led economic development plans have been directly reflected in education policy and planning. The government has been generally successful in providing and expanding the education system based on the industrial needs for human resources. As a result, the education system has developed in tandem with the various stages of economic development. The focus of the government's educational plan has moved from primary to secondary education and finally to the tertiary level, according to the nation's economic advancement. The rapid expansion of education in terms of quantity, and to a lesser extent quality, is the most salient feature of South Korean educational development during the country's industrialisation.

Since South Korea launched an economic development programme early in the 1960s, industrialisation and urbanisation have continued to accelerate. With little natural resources available, South Korea's strong family structure and high respect for education

South Korea

have been the driving force behind the country's economic development. South Koreans' strong belief in education is attributed in large measure to the emphasis on credentials that prevails in the society. Education has also played a major role in laying the foundation upon which democratic principles and institutions are based. It has promoted political knowledge, changed political behaviour patterns, and shaped political attitudes and values. At the same time, education has imbued the people with commitment to modernisation and citizenship. Increased educational opportunities have made upward social mobility possible, and the middle class has expanded as a result.

The formal education system follows a single track of six years in elementary school, three years in middle school, three years in high school, and four years in college or university. Elementary education is free and compulsory. Upon reaching the age of six, children receive a notification of admission to a school in their residential area. Upon entrance to elementary school, children automatically advance to the next grade each year. Free, compulsory middle-school education began in 1985 in farming and fishing areas and was gradually expanded nationwide. Middle-school graduates have two options: to attend an academic general high school or a vocational high school. Those who are admitted to a vocational high school cannot transfer to an academic high school. But there is no restriction on vocational high school graduates entering higher education institutions. Therefore, overall student selection and screening are reserved until candidates are selected for universities and colleges.

Everyone is encouraged to participate in the competition for higher education. This system of contested mobility resulted in a continuous increase in the demand for educational opportunities and thus pushed the government to extend the provision of such opportunities.

The education system has been successful at the primary and secondary levels in providing equal educational access to students, irrespective of their gender, geographical location and socio-economic background. The rate of pupil retention is nearly 100% in the lower grades.

Table 5
Gross enrolment ratios by gender, South Korea (2005)

Level of education	% female	% male
Primary	104	105
Middle	96	95
High	90	90
Tertiary	69	110

Source: Kim and Rhee (2007)

South Korea's education system at school level has achieved quality improvements in tandem with quantitative expansion. For example, the most recent published results (2003) (Kim & Rhee 2007) of periodic international tests in mathematics and science, such as the OECD's Programme for International Student Assessment (PISA) and Trends in International Mathematics and Science Study (TIMSS), provided the evidence for the highly competitive knowledge and skills of 15-year-old students. In the 2003 PISA, South Korea finished third behind Hong Kong and Finland on mathematics and science scores, and in TIMSS, second behind Singapore (Kim & Rhee 2007: 110–113).

Similarly, the 'efficiency index' shows that the efficiency of secondary education in South Korea ranks second to Finland among OECD countries. This index is calculated by running the regression of reading literacy of the 15-year-old students on the cumulative expenditure per pupil for children aged six through fifteen. The result indicates that South Korean students show relatively high performance, although South Korea's cumulative expenditures per pupil are below the OECD average.

When compared to the average high-income country, South Korea also stands up relatively well. It performs relatively better in terms of the quality of mathematics and science education, internet access in schools, tertiary enrolment, and average years of schooling. On the other hand, it is relatively weaker in the quality of management schools, brain drain and the availability of professional and technical workers.

Despite larger classes, South Korean pupils' achievement levels have been very high, compared to those in other OECD countries, as shown in international comparisons of student achievement such as PISA and TIMSS (Kim & Rhee 2007). Considering that the numbers of students per teacher and per class in South Korea are higher, the South Korean education system can be judged to be efficient, at least at the primary and secondary levels. This implies that South Korean teachers were able to provide high-quality education according to international standards, despite larger class sizes and, therefore, much lower cost per student.

A key factor here was the decision by the South Korean government to provide diverse incentives to recruit competent people for the teaching profession. Until 1990, public colleges charged no tuition for teacher training. Job security was another factor in recruiting high-quality young people for the teaching profession, especially in times of rapid economic and labour market restructuring. This phenomenon can be clearly observed in the increasing number of high school graduates with high scores applying for teacher colleges.

Main features of educational development
In the late 1940s and 1950s, education policy focused on establishing educational infrastructure and expanding primary and secondary education, which are critical to supplying industry with a skilled workforce. The most conspicuous feature of educational development in the 1960s was the quantitative expansion of student enrolment and the number of schools. Vocational high schools were established to provide training in craft skills for the growing labour-intensive light industries. During the 1970s, one of the priority areas of economic development plans was the strengthening of vocational education. Vocational junior colleges were set up to supply technicians for the heavy and chemical industries.

The rate of educational expansion is more remarkable at the tertiary level. Until the 1970s, the college admission quota was strictly regulated by the government, which set up the

South Korea

quota based on the analysis of the demand for human resources. However, in 1980, the government abolished college entrance examinations and expanded educational opportunities for higher education. During the 1990s, the government initiated diversification and specialisation of higher education institutions to accommodate the diverse needs of society. For this purpose, standards and conditions for granting university charters were loosened, and the numbers of institutions and of students increased steeply after 1996.

During the 1970s and 1980s, higher education was expanded in two ways: increased student enrolment and diversified institutions of higher education. As junior colleges took a larger share of tertiary education, their programmes were diversified to meet industrial needs. Education reform in the 1980s included such measures as abolishing university entrance examinations, renovating school facilities, and introducing incentives for teachers. The availability of human resources became increasingly strained in the 1980s. The growth of the economically active population dropped sharply in that decade compared to the previous decade, and labour demand continued to increase as the economy grew at a high average annual rate of 10% in the second half of the 1980s. The changes in labour demand toward a more skilled and high-calibre workforce in the 1980s – brought about by the rapid economic growth – called for strengthening science and engineering education in universities.

The rapid economic growth had a strong effect on human resource development in two ways. On the industrial side, rapid industrialisation affected skill formation in workplaces; in particular, industrial deepening in a short time required substantial efforts to upgrade workforce skills and knowledge. On the supply side, the education and training system needed to change to meet the new requirements of the industry. Hence, South Korea's education and training system responded to the growth of the South Korean economy through rapid expansion of student enrolment capacity, which caused the imbalance between quantitative expansion and qualitative improvement of education and the skill mismatch between public training and industrial needs.

Key success factors and limitations of previous development
Education has played an important role in South Korea's successful industrialisation. However, the government-led, supply-side educational policy and planning caused rigidity in the education and training systems and an imbalance between quantitative expansion and qualitative improvement, which turned out to be serious constraints to South Korea's transition to a knowledge-based economy.

In 1968, the government abolished the middle-school entrance examination and instead introduced a system of student allocation in which primary-school graduates were assigned to a middle-school system through a lottery system. With the elimination of the middle-school entrance examination, the flow of students into and out of the middle-school system greatly increased and, consequently, competition for entrance into the elite high schools became severe. In 1974, the government again responded by adopting the High School Equalization Policy, which was intended to make every high school equal in terms of students' academic background, educational conditions, teaching staff and financing. A new admissions policy, which is still in effect in metropolitan areas, replaced each individual high school's entrance exam with a locally administered standardised test and a lottery system. The abolition of the secondary entrance examinations brought about a great increase in secondary education opportunities.

Higher education expanded rapidly in the mid-1950s because of the government's laissez-faire policy regarding increases in enrolment quotas. The aim of the policy was to accommodate the demand for higher education, which was suppressed during Japanese rule. However, the laissez-faire policy resulted in the over-supply of and high unemployment rates among college graduates. The government then exercised tight control over the enrolment quotas for each college and university. As a result, college enrolment increased slowly until the 1970s. During the 1970s, the government selectively expanded the enrolment quotas in the fields of engineering, natural sciences, business and commerce, and foreign languages, but it basically maintained the policy of slow expansion. Higher education greatly expanded during the first half of the 1980s under a policy of adopting a graduation enrolment quota system and expanding enrolment quotas. Higher education continued to expand during the 1990s. The main areas of expansion were two-year vocational colleges and fields of engineering and natural sciences at four-year colleges and universities.

In general, the government's expansion policy for higher education has been effective in terms of supplying highly-qualified white-collar workers and R&D personnel according to each stage of economic development. Specifically, the government's control over the enrolment quotas during the 1960s and 1970s played a key role in balancing the demand and supply of college graduates in the labour market, consequently reducing inefficiency in the national economy and social problems that resulted from the over-supply and underemployment of college graduates. However, the demands of an increasingly globalised and knowledge-based economy have exposed the shortfalls in the quality of the outputs from the higher education system and the ability of graduates to cope with the demands of the labour market.

Education financing

Over the years, the growth rates of the education budget have outpaced those of the GDP, and the government has put a high priority on education spending over the years. From 1963 to 2005, the government's spending on education increased more than 29 times in real terms, while the GDP and the government's overall budget increased 20 times (Kim & Rhee 2007: 117).

The share of the education budget out of total government budget had remained at around 15% in 1960, but increased over the years reaching more than 20% in the 2000s (Kim & Rhee 2007: 117).

For secondary and higher education, a substantial amount of funding comes from the private sector, such as households and private foundations. At the secondary level, the private share is more than 40%, and at the tertiary level, it is over 70% (Kim &

South Korea

Rhee 2007: 117). Because of budget constraints, the government encouraged private foundations to establish secondary schools and higher education institutions. Expenses for school operation were funded through user fees. Private financing therefore accounts for about two-thirds of total direct costs in education. Also, households in South Korea cover much more of the education costs (76.7%) than do their counterparts in most European countries, which is on average about 21.4% (Kim & Rhee 2007: 117).

The net effect of educational expansion between 1965 and 1990 showed that secondary school enrolment and investment in education had a positive relationship to South Korea's economic growth. Expansion of secondary school enrolment and public investment in secondary education were very important in offsetting diminishing returns on investment in physical capital; thus, the investment in education contributed significantly to sustaining the growth of per capita income. Human capital investment has been successful from an economic point of view: it has enabled the timely supply of human resources and offset the diminishing returns to physical capital investment.

Private funding for education

Primary education in South Korea has been treated as a collective good, and it has been mostly publicly-funded (see Tables 6 and 7). The heavy reliance on private funding in secondary and higher education has an important policy implication. Inducing the private sector to play a more active role in providing educational services at the secondary and higher educational levels would offer a leverage effect, allowing limited government resources to be spent on prioritised areas. Until recent years, by leaving higher levels of education to the private sector and targeting public resources for primary education, South Korea has been able to address one of the main equity issues: basic education for all.

Table 6
Ratio of private to national/public institutions, South Korea (2005)

Education level	National/public	Private
Colleges and universities	15.6	84.4
High schools	55.8	95.0
Middle schools	77.3	22.7
Primary schools	98.7	1.3

Source: Kim and Rhee (2007)

Table 7
Enrolment ratio of private to national/public institutions, South Korea (2005)

Education level	National/public	Private
Colleges and universities	25.5	74.5
High schools	51.0	49.0
Middle schools	80.9	19.1
Primary schools	98.8	1.2

Source: Kim and Rhee (2007)

While there is little doubt that increased private involvement in tertiary education has enabled the release of public resources for the universalisation of high-quality basic education, at the same time it has reduced the leverage of the state to influence the outcomes of tertiary education in line with the needs for further economic and social development.

The central government has also supported private-school foundations through tax benefits. For example, private-school foundations are regarded as non-profit organisations, so they can save on corporation tax, which for-profit organisations cannot do, and they are allowed to receive tax-exempt donations and endowments. In addition to these benefits, governments have promoted private schools through loan systems. The Korean Foundation for the Promotion of Private Schools was established in 1989 to support private schools in improving the educational environment. Long-term loans with low interest rates are provided for private schools at any level. The Foundation and its loans have turned out to be so successful that even given the limited financial resources at the government level, the education sector has expanded rapidly with the help of private resources.

While there are no official data or other information, anecdotal evidence gathered during interviews conducted during the visit suggests that many private tertiary education institutions are de facto for-profit institutions.

The higher education system

As a result of expansion that has occurred over the last 20 years, South Korea now has the highest rate of participation in tertiary education of any country, with the possible exception of Finland (Grubb *et al.* 2006). This remarkable expansion, which has been achieved almost entirely through increased rates of progression of students from upper secondary education to the tertiary level, has been the result of several factors. These include the expansion of upper secondary education, whose completion rates are now also among the highest in the world. In turn these high completion rates have been made possible by very high levels of achievement in literacy, mathematics and science. Helping to drive both of these expansions in educational participation has been a traditional South Korean zeal for education. Within the tertiary education system itself, much of the explanation for the expansion can be found in a loosening of the regulations governing the establishment of new institutions, and a heavy reliance upon private funding (Grubb *et al.* 2006).

South Korea, like many other countries, emphasises the role of formal schooling for its value in creating economic growth, international competitiveness and individual advancement. The current goals of the South Korean government for tertiary education are largely related to economic development, including increasing the international competitiveness of tertiary education, improving the employment rates of graduates, increasing knowledge transfer between industry and academia, providing education that better prepares students for the demands of industry, and building 15 world-calibre research universities.

In 1945, when South Korea was liberated from Japanese rule, there was only one national university. Seven national universities were established during the period 1951–1953. The modern system of universities in South Korea is therefore little more than 50 years old.

The period between 1960 and 1980 was largely concerned with economic development and the links of education to economic growth, marked by an emphasis on science and the establishment of vocational schools (now colleges). The real expansion of universities and colleges took place initially during the 1960s, but also during the 1980s when there was a 30% increase in student numbers, and during the 1990s. Legislation passed in 1995 facilitated the establishment of new universities and two-year colleges. Between 1990 and 2004, the number of tertiary institutions increased from 265 to 411; the number of students from 1.7 million to 3.5 million; the number of faculty from 42 911 to 66 862; and the number of administrative staff from 32 613 to 38 457 (Grubb *et al*, 2006). (South Africa, whose population is of a similar size to that of South Korea, has only 23 public universities and 127 private higher education institutions).

In addition, the completion rate of secondary school increased, from 46% in 1970 to almost 100% by 1999 (Grubb *et al*. 2006: 6). South Korea has thereby become one of the first countries to have nearly universal completion of secondary education. Currently, 81% of all secondary-school graduates go on to tertiary education (Grubb *et al*. 2006: 7).

Universities of many kinds dominate tertiary education and provide four-year programmes leading to a baccalaureate degree. The majority of universities are nominally private, with government-sponsored (national or public) universities enrolling only 22% of university students. National universities receive governmental funding, are administered by the Ministry of Education and, in a few cases, by other ministries. Private universities depend more on tuition fee revenues, and their tuition fee levels are typically higher. They are more autonomous and governed by a corporate board, although they are also subject to a variety of Ministry of Education regulations.

In 2003, national universities received 62% of their funds from the government, 30% from student fees, and 8% from other sources. Private institutions, on the other hand, received 69% of their revenue from tuition fees (Grubb *et al*. 2006: 8).

Most universities are comprehensive, providing teaching in a broad range of sciences, social sciences, the humanities, and professional subjects like engineering and business. However, some are limited to technical subjects; for example, the Korea Advanced Institute of Science and Technology (KAIST), and the Pohang University of Science and Technology (POSTECH) founded by the Pohang Iron and Steel Company, are high-quality, high-status universities largely devoted to engineering subjects.

While most universities are under the control of the Ministry of Education, other ministries have created universities: KAIST is funded partly by the Ministry of Science and Technology; and, the Korean University of Technology and Education has been funded by the Ministry of Labour, originally to train teachers for labour market programmes. Particularly with the expansion of universities after 1990, there was great scope for institutional differentiation; however, this has not happened with the university system as a whole, providing little choice to students. In other words, there is great potential for differentiation, but up to now little has been seen in practice.

Table 8
Number of institutions and students by type of institution, South Korea (2004)

Education level	National/public		Private		Total	
	Institutions	Students	Institutions	Students	Institutions	Students
University	26	397 352	145	1 439 297	171	1 836 649
Junior College	15	38 747	143	858 842	158	897 589
University Of Education	11	23 335			11	22 335
Industrial University	8	86 892	10	102 143	18	189 035
Technical University			1	196	1	196
Open University	1	290 728			1	290 728
Cyber University			17	39 450	17	39 450
Corporate University			1	62	1	62
Grad School University			28	276 918	28	276 918
Miscellaneous Schools			5	1 153	5	1 153
Total	61	921 046	350	2 634 069	411	3 555 115

Source: Grubb *et al.* (2006)

The second dominant type of institution is the college, which now enrols about 40% of students in tertiary education. Most programmes last two years, though about 10% of students are enrolled in three-year programmes, especially in the sciences, engineering and other technical fields. These institutions exist to prepare middle-level human resources and technicians. The fields of study include a range of occupations in engineering, health (including nursing), business and law, and education.

Compared to universities, a much larger fraction of colleges and college enrolments are in private rather than national institutions. This in turn means that those institutions are more reliant on tuition fees and less on government funding. They also do not receive government funding for research, as some universities do. On the other hand, colleges appear to be more closely related to employers than universities are: it is more common for colleges to set up partnerships with local firms, and they often offer customised training in which firms pay for short-term training adapted or customised to their purposes.

Colleges are characterised by their lower status, compared to universities. Most students will not consider applying to colleges if they have a chance to attend a university, and some companies will not hire from colleges. In addition, university graduates have been taking jobs that colleges generally prepare their students for, so in some ways colleges are being squeezed out of their major labour markets.

Higher education challenges

The higher education system in South Korea faces many challenges, including:

- Labour market responsiveness
- Public financing

- Quality
- Research, and
- Equity.

Labour market responsiveness

A key challenge is to improve the linkages between tertiary education and the labour market. While it is often asserted that more individuals need to be schooled to meet the challenges of competition and growth, there is evidence that the rapid expansion of tertiary education has resulted in over-education. In addition, there are complaints, particularly from employers, that the skills of graduates do not match the skills required in the labour market (Grubb *et al.* 2006).

Box 6
Korea Research Institute for Vocational Education and Training (KRIVET)

KRIVET is a national policy research organisation located under the Office of the Prime Minister. It was founded in 1997 to support the development of national human resources policy, and the lifelong vocational competency development of South Koreans. Among the functions it undertakes are the following:

- R&D on national human resources development policy
- R&D on lifelong learning and lifelong vocational education and training policy
- R&D on the qualifications system
- Development of vocational education and training programmes
- Projects related to the evaluation of vocational education and training institutes, and assessment and approval of vocational education and training programmes
- Research and projects related to vocational career information, and
- International cooperation and exchange projects in human resource development and vocational education and training.

One of the most important functions carried out by KRIVET is the labour market tracking of students who have received vocational education and training in order to determine, inter alia, whether their occupation and earnings are in line with their training.

South Korea is struggling to produce sufficient numbers of science and engineering graduates. The trend among students is to shun science and engineering majors. Furthermore, those who do enter these fields often leave South Korea to pursue their careers. There are several distinct types of mismatches in the labour market. These include the problems of over-education, rather than a shortage of skilled workers; the potential under-supply of trade workers; the complaints of employers about the skills of recent graduates; and the overall flexibility of the existing system in responding to changes in employment (Grubb *et al.* 2006).

There is some evidence that the real problem in South Korea is an over-supply of individuals with baccalaureate, and probably associate, degrees. Graduates are having problems getting the kinds of skilled professional and managerial jobs they expect. In many cases, students have taken a 'leave of absence'; that is, they take periods off from their studies rather than enter the labour market as graduates with low probability of success. Furthermore, there is a general consensus that university graduates have taken jobs that were designed for college graduates – sometimes because university graduates simply apply for these jobs when they are unable to get better jobs, but sometimes because universities have opened baccalaureate programmes that explicitly compete with college programmes.

Similarly, as college graduates have faced competition from university graduates, they have begun to fill jobs that previously were filled by graduates of secondary vocational schools. Thus, the employment rates of college graduates are higher than those of university graduates, but their average earnings are not much higher than those of high school graduates. In contrast, those with a Bachelors degree earn considerably more. Enrolment in college thus appears to be a route to more stable and higher-status employment, but not to higher earnings.

The process of over-education, where university graduates have displaced college graduates who in turn have displaced secondary school graduates, together with the intense pressure to attend tertiary education, has led to apparent shortages of trade-level workers – the electricians, plumbers, mechanics and secretaries required for construction, assembly lines and modern corporations. Although these occupations are supposedly prepared for in vocational secondary schools, these institutions now send 62% of their graduates to tertiary education (up from only 8% in 1990) (Grubb *et al.* 2006: 22) so they are no longer predominantly 'terminal' institutions providing vocational education for the mid-level workforce.

However, there has been little recognition that over-education in tertiary education has been matched by some under-education for jobs for which secondary schools have traditionally prepared students – for example, construction workers and tradespeople like electricians and plumbers.

The process of over-education is caused by at least two different phenomena. One is the desire of students and their parents for higher levels of schooling, and schooling of the highest possible reputation, in order to get the best jobs. But educational institutions themselves have also been responsible for over-education. When the government allowed the founding of more institutions in the 1990s, enormous numbers of universities were founded. And there appears to be pressure by several different education and training institutions to provide higher-level degrees.

Overall, the expansion of tertiary education seems to have outpaced the demand for jobs requiring high levels of schooling. Furthermore, the dominant economic incentives in the current system are to enhance the numbers of those with baccalaureate degrees, while the incentives for completing associate degrees are weak. It seems likely that the South Korean system is preparing too few technicians in colleges, while there are too many individuals with baccalaureate degrees who cannot find appropriate employment.

A second potential problem with labour market linkages relates to whether graduates have inadequate skills, even among those who have graduated from universities and colleges. In addition to general concerns about skills shortages in areas of strategic national

South Korea

importance, employers also complain about the lack of appropriate skills such as problem-solving and the ability to perform well in groups, among the young people they hire.

A different type of mismatch involves the overall flexibility of tertiary education in response to labour market changes. If an education system is intended to prepare workers, then enrolment patterns should change as occupational patterns change. This is particularly important in countries like South Korea, with open economies subject to variation in international trade, and to countries trying to compete by developing new technologies. However, in South Korea, the flexibility and responsiveness of tertiary education has been limited by funding allocations based on an extrapolation of historical demand patterns in the context of a quota system, which establishes limits on enrolments in the Seoul area, as well as limiting enrolments in the fields of medicine and teacher education. The most obvious evidence of this is the stability in enrolment patterns in universities over the past ten years, even as demand in certain sectors (like health and engineering) has been increasing. Given the dominance of private financing of higher education, there is little the government can do to 'steer' the higher education system towards producing the types of human resources needed by the economy.

Public financing
In South Korea only 0.5% of GDP is spent by government on higher education, as opposed to the 1% OECD average (Grubb *et al.* 2006: 15). As stated earlier, the fact that the higher education system is dominated by private financing has important implications for economic development because it is evident that the private component of the higher education system is not producing sufficient numbers of high-quality graduates for the increasingly sophisticated economy. The extent of private involvement in higher education is staggering. For example, almost all of the 200 or so colleges are private; 145 out of 171 universities are private (85%); and 75% of students are in private institutions (Grubb *et al.* 2006: 7).

Quality
There is general agreement in South Korea that expansion has resulted in lower quality. However, there is little agreement on what to do about it. Furthermore, the country's quality assurance mechanisms appear relatively weak, both at the system and institutional levels.

Research
A distinctive feature of R&D in South Korea is the strong role played by private companies. In the context of a national concern to improve the contribution of R&D to economic performance, this raises key questions about the role that tertiary education should play in national research policies.

The emphasis upon knowledge-intensive industries within national economic policy results in high priority being attached to R&D; to science and innovation policies; to the development of advanced technologies such as wireless broadband, digital multimedia broadcasting and robotics; and to policies that can turn knowledge into commercial products with a competitive advantage.

The following are two key indicators of South Korea's national innovation system (Suh & Chen 2007):

- R&D expenditure increased from USD9 million in 1969 (73% public) to USD24 billion in 2006 (75% private).
- The number of researchers increased from 5 337 in 1969 to 256 598 in 2006; 7% in government, 26% at university and 68% in private sector.

What these statistics reveal is that the rate of growth of investment in R&D was extremely high between the 1960s and the 2000s, but that the nature of that investment has shifted dramatically from being dominated by the public sector in the 1960s to overwhelming dominance by the private sector by the 2000s. In line with this changing investment pattern, more than two-thirds of researchers are employed in the private sector. South Korea has become concerned with R&D as a way of enhancing technology and competitiveness, and a persistent question is what the role of tertiary institutions in R&D should be. Up to now, higher education institutions have played little or no role in R&D in the national innovation system.

In terms of the volume of overall R&D, South Korean universities play a relatively small role. About 76% of overall spending on R&D is carried out by corporations, 14% is carried out by research institutes, and only 10% is done in universities – a proportion that has increased only slightly over the past decade, from about 7% in 1993 (Grubb *et al.* 2006: 49). Given the prominent role of firms in R&D in South Korea, it is unlikely that in the foreseeable future universities will become major players, particularly since a great deal of current R&D funded by firms is intended to develop new products – a firm-specific and market-driven form of R&D that is less appropriate for universities.

Virtually all corporate research funding (95%) goes to corporate R&D. Of government funding, the majority (52%) goes to research institutes, 19% to corporate efforts and 29% to universities – the latter largely to research universities (67%) rather than to teaching-orientated universities (30%). Most of the research funding to teaching-oriented universities (7%) goes to institutions located outside of Seoul, suggesting that these funds are being used to strengthen these institutions. In contrast, most of the funds to research universities (66%) goes to institutions within Seoul. Overall, 67% of government research funds go to the top 20 universities, including a couple of institutions outside Seoul (particularly KAIST and POSTECH), so that only a very few universities have meaningful amounts of research funding (Grubb *et al.* 2006).

Overall then, the role of universities in national R&D is quite small. However, there are two roles in which universities are particularly important. One is the support of basic research, as distinct from commercial research. While universities carried out only 10% of overall R&D, university faculty contributed 76% of the scientific papers written in South Korea. The second role relates to the training of potential researchers in which universities naturally have a predominant role.

South Korea

A recent OECD review (Grubb *et al.* 2006) concluded that the two most useful roles of universities in R&D are: (1) to engage in basic research, some of which might be motivated by potential (but uncertain) commercial applications; and (2) to prepare the next generation of researchers through the development of more extensive postgraduate programmes. In terms of basic research, its connection to commercial applications is enhanced when universities maintain ties with corporations. Currently there appear to be many such ties: every university has a university–industry liaison office supported by government funds, and the co-worker system promotes joint research between university and corporation researchers. In addition, there is some joint support between the Ministry of Education, the Ministry of Commerce, the Ministry of Science and Technology, and the Ministry of Information and Communications – though apparently this collaboration has achieved only limited results. These ties should surely be continued and strengthened.

Equity

Unlike in schooling, in higher education, with respect to equity, there are serious concerns with regard to gender, class and region. Gender differences in tertiary participation are relatively marked, and are linked to the overall role of women in South Korean society and the labour market. For example, there are concerns about the ability of women to progress to tertiary education – only 20% of South Korean women aged 25–64 have a tertiary qualification, compared to 32% of men of the same age (Grubb *et al.* 2006: 57). (See Table 4 for gender differences in participation rates).

The rapid expansion of tertiary education has led to various possibilities related to equity. On the one hand, the expansion has opened up more places in colleges and universities, and these should have enhanced the ability of lower-income students and women to attend. On the other hand, the expansion of tertiary education has been accompanied largely by expanding places in new and therefore lower-status universities, and in colleges. This means that lower-income students and women might have gained access to lower-status institutions, including those that do not lead to postgraduate education.

In order to enhance equity, South Korea has a number of grants, loans and other outreach programmes that are intended to enhance the access of low-income students and women to private universities. In addition, the Ministry of Education uses its control over the admissions process to try to influence equity, though whether this approach is successful is unclear.

Many universities and colleges use fee waivers (grants) to attract students they want to admit, waiving some or all of the tuition fees they normally charge. Some universities, including a few of the highest-status universities, use tuition waivers and special admissions procedures to allow low-income students to enter, but most fee waivers appear to be merit-based; that is, they are efforts by universities to attract the 'best' (or highest-scoring) students. Such mechanisms work against equity.

In addition, South Korea has an extensive system of loans: there are eight major loan programmes – administered by the Ministry of Education, the Ministry of Labour, the Korean Labour Welfare Corporation, the Government Employees Pension Cooperative, and the Korean Teachers Pension – aimed at different groups of students (with some limited to science and engineering majors, or victims of work-related accidents, or workers), with different interest rates and repayment schedules. These are available to students in universities and postgraduate schools, but not to college students.

In addition, a number of special programmes exist to admit students with certain kinds of social disadvantage. Again, there is a large number of small programmes, for groups like housewives, children of sailors and accident victims, and students from farming and fishing communities, but overall these apply to about 50 000 students while close to 400 000 students are accepted each year (Grubb *et al.* 2006: 58).

The OECD review (Grubb *et al.* 2006) has described the equity mechanisms in South Korea as 'haphazard', with different institutions having different goals. There are too many loan programmes, uncoordinated and with different repayment options, to understand easily, and the resulting effects on discouraging attendance are unknown. There are funds intended to enhance the equity of attending universities and colleges, but nothing to enhance equity of access, which is seriously influenced by private tutoring in high school.

The expansion of tertiary education in South Korea should certainly have enhanced opportunities for the children of low-income families to take part in tertiary study. There is, however, an association between family background and the types of institutions in which young people enrol, with those from low-income families being more likely to attend the less prestigious and often lower-quality institutions.

University–industry linkages

As stated earlier, historically there has been poor interaction between universities and business with respect to research and innovation. One reason is that most large firms have built up their own training and education facilities. However, given the increasing demands of a knowledge-based economy, the need for a national innovation system based on greater cooperation between government research agencies, universities and the private sector appears to be paramount.

A number of initiatives have been started to facilitate this process. In an effort to foster proactive collaboration and create a channel for communicating the demands and needs of industry to the education community, the government is formulating a new industry-academia collaboration system, which is based on the Act on the Promotion of Industrial Education and Industry–Academia Collaboration (Kim & Rhee 2007). Taking into consideration the diverse regional characteristics and unique circumstances of universities and industries, the Ministry of Education has classified cases of industry-academia collaboration into three groups (see Types 1, 2 and 3 in Table 9 below). Policy implementation and financial support will be closely tied to the collaborative system to eventually create a university system that fully incorporates the industry–academia collaboration framework.

South Korea

In addition to financial support, the government introduced two new features into the higher education system. One is a contract-based education system that enables close ties between industry and academia. This system has been established to allow the needs of the industrial sector to be directly reflected in the operation of the university curriculum. For example, new majors as well as departments can be established under contract between universities and private enterprises. The contract can stipulate matters related to the student quota, student selection process, curriculum, teaching and learning processes, and so forth. Upon graduation, students enrolled in the programme will receive favourable employment opportunities from the companies. The other feature is a school-enterprise system that enables the practical application of the research conducted through the industry-academia collaboration.

The link between universities and industry is expected to get stronger with the establishment of a new regional governance system, the Regional Innovation Committee (consisting of key stakeholders in each major city and province), to facilitate communication among the key stakeholders. Financial support from both central and local governments is available; however, the collaboration among them is not as active as expected. The types of collaboration expected from this process are depicted in Table 9.

Table 9
Types of collaboration between industry and academia in South Korea

Type 1	Human resources endowed with world-class research and development capabilities: • Project to upgrade universities that conduct research in their graduate schools, turning them into research centres. • Project to support academic research environment.
Type 2	Human resources for hi-tech development: • Innovation project (NURI) to reinforce the capabilities of universities outside the Seoul metropolitan area and vicinity. • Project for the specialisation of universities in the Seoul metropolitan area.
Type 3	Human resources for industrial technology: • Selection of universities by each region to be industry-academia collaboration universities. • Project to identify unique characteristics of junior colleges.

Concluding observations and implications for African countries

The changing higher education scene

South Korea's education system has responded well to the basic educational needs of the population and was successful in delivering the human resources required for South Korea's industrialisation efforts. However, the rapid quantitative expansion of the higher education system resulted in a lowering of quality, and limited diversity and relevance. In that policy context, the higher educational institutions have not been able to provide the quality of human resources to flexibly meet the changing socio-economic demand in a knowledge-based economy.

The Presidential Commission on Education of 1995 clearly spelt out the challenges:

> *Korean education, having registered a marked growth in quantitative terms*
> *in the era of industrialisation, will no longer be appropriate in the era of*

information technology and globalisation. It will not be able to produce persons who possess high levels of creativity and moral sensitivity, which are required to sharpen the nation's competitive edge in the coming era. (KEDI 2005: 1)

Since the 1960s, South Korea has been able to achieve high economic growth by increasing the input of labour and capital, which required the government to play an active role. In this government-led strategy, based on the growth of large-scale industry, the government has been highly interventionist. The approach has been reflected also in South Korea's educational development process. Rigid government control over the education system included the curriculum, examination system, tuition fees, number of students, and so forth, for both public and private schools. The result of these top-down education policies has been the loss of autonomy and lack of accountability by individual institutions.

Consequently, strategic partnerships and connections among knowledge-producing institutions such as corporations, universities and research institutions, along with institutional and organisational structures that govern such partnerships, are weak. Such systemic weakness is also found in the international exchange of people and knowledge, such as the establishment of foreign universities and research institutions and inadequate participation in joint international research projects. In addition, the brain drain from South Korea has accelerated with the increased international competition for highly skilled workers.

Universities have focused on the traditional mission of training scholars and the leaders of society. They have remained passive in the practical application of knowledge and failed to respond effectively to job-market realities. The universities have not succeeded in specialising in a manner that reflects the uniqueness of local industry and culture. Consequently, their role as a centre for creating and disseminating knowledge in the local community has remained weak. Therefore, the training of high-quality human resources and the acquisition of advanced technology have relied on such alternative means as overseas education.

Owing to the expansion of compulsory education and the universalisation of higher education, the quantitative basis for supplying human resources is relatively strong. In contrast, the educational environment has not improved, with the quality of university education and the capabilities of university research remaining poor.

South Korea has a large pool of highly educated workers. More than 80% of high school graduates go on to higher education, but there is a problem of imbalance between academic fields. Professional schools, including law and medical schools, are much preferred to the science and engineering faculties. But there is an increasing demand for college students who will develop the core competencies needed in the knowledge-based economy of the 21st century. It is, however, evident that South Korean universities are not improving college students' competencies in critical thinking, communication, self-motivated learning, leadership, problem-solving or cooperation.

There is, however, increasing evidence that the South Korean education system is responding to these demands. Primary and secondary education focus more now on

South Korea

excellence and creativity than on generality, and tertiary education provides competitive, high-quality education and research. The expanded private system is expected to provide greater coherence with the needs of the labour market. In that context, South Korea's education policy and system have been progressing from the past industrial model toward a knowledge-based model since the mid-1990s.

Current reforms and new initiatives

Some key policy lessons can be drawn from the South Korean experience in developing skills and human resources for the knowledge-based economy. These include the following:

- Education and training are critical
- Education and training need to be relevant to the particular needs of industries and various sectors of the economy, and
- Education and training need to develop over time to keep pace with the changing needs of the economy.

There is some evidence that higher education is drawing more attention and importance in government education policies as the economy is transformed toward a knowledge-based economy. A clear shift has occurred, with government increasing its spending on the higher education sector more than on primary and secondary education. This policy change is caused by two factors. On the one hand, because the government recognises the quality of human resources as the key factor in further economic growth, it regards the higher education sector as the key player in achieving that growth. On the other hand, the performance of the current higher education system in South Korea is perceived to be lower than expected in terms of the efficiency of educational spending.

Higher education institutions have insisted that they must have a high degree of freedom from external intervention and of control to perform effectively. The government has steadily carried out such regulatory reforms in higher education since the mid-1990s.

The main thrust of recent regulatory reforms in higher education is to make the institutions more entrepreneurial and responsive by granting a greater level of autonomy in setting the number of students to be admitted, hiring teaching staff, and managing academic affairs. For example, until 1998, the number of students admitted to colleges and universities was determined by the government, based on educational conditions such as student-faculty ratio and human resources requirements at the national level. Beginning in 1999, private universities, with the exception of medical schools, teachers' colleges and universities located in and around the Seoul metropolitan area, were allowed to determine the number of administrative personnel or professors by submitting a proposal stating their standards and plans. Regulatory reforms in the late 1990s also resulted in allowing foreigners to become professors at national public universities, opening the doors to high-quality human resources from abroad. Since 2002, colleges and universities have been permitted to set the amount of tuition fees, depending on each university's specific financial situation.

South Korea has achieved a stage of mass higher education, but it is not easy to see any differences among colleges and universities. Because most institutions of higher learning are interested in quantitative expansion, they underestimate the important missions given to them, such as quality assurance and specialisation in unique characteristics. Now, similar departments, colleges and graduate programmes can be easily found in almost all universities.

As a sign of its intention to promote restructuring for efficiency, the government announced a University Restructuring Plan in 2004 (KEDI 2005). The key objectives of the plan are to:

- Lay the foundation for improving the quality of higher education beyond the growth in quantity
- Improve the efficiency of tertiary education investment
- Develop human resources that meet the needs of society, and
- Support development of South Korean universities to become world-class institutions.

To achieve these goals, the government provided W80 billion to 23 institutions of higher education in 2005 and will continue to support them until 2008 if they maintain their qualifications for the project (KEDI 2005: 2). In addition to the financial incentives, colleges and universities undergoing restructuring or downsizing will be given favourable credits on applications for government-funded higher education projects, such as Brain Korea 21 (BK21) and the New University for Regional Innovation (NURI) (see below).

Although it is too early to tell whether the government's university-restructuring initiatives will succeed, a fair number of colleges and universities are in the process of restructuring and downsizing. In 2005, eight national colleges and universities in local provinces were consolidated into four universities, and 38 institutions of higher education announced their intention to downsize their enrolments by about 10% over the next three years (KEDI 2005: 3). Nevertheless, it remains to be seen whether the institutions of higher education will be able to become more distinctive.

New initiative 1: Upgrading research capability
Until recent years, most applied research has been left to government research institutes and the private sector. The higher education institutions were, in general, not really interested in or willing to build up competencies in engineering and science. To strengthen the research capacity of universities, the Ministry of Education set up a plan suggesting two large projects: the second phase of BK21, and the Five-Year Plan for the Development of Basic Sciences. South Korea's aim for the two projects was to have about 15 universities with world-class reputations by 2010. The post-BK21 will be more focused on science and technology, whereas the Five-Year Plan is for the humanities and social sciences. The former project is being planned in close cooperation with the ministries dealing with hi-tech or national strategic industries, with consideration of the industries' inter-sectoral character.

South Korea

A very important feature of BK21 is that it rates and supports departments or research units, not individual academics, since it believes that research progress is made in teams. An important aspect of rating the team is that it must have international participation and it gets marks for relevance and disadvantage.

Box 7
Brain Korea 21

BK21 is a national human resource development project that aims to fulfil the demand for high-quality human resources which South Korea will need to thrive in the fierce competition of the knowledge-based society of the 21st century. The ultimate objective of the project is to meet the needs of the times for creative and high-quality R&D human resources.

The seven-year project, which started in 1999, has contributed greatly to improving the research capability of universities and developing excellent human resources. Universities involved in BK21 have changed their administrative systems and improved student selection methods to move toward becoming research-orientated institutions. For example, they enhanced research capability by introducing pay-for-performance based on professors' research achievements, thus creating a favourable environment for research.

The second phase of the BK21 project began in February 2006, and is scheduled to continue until 2012. Based on the research infrastructure built during the first phase of the project and the 'selection and concentration' strategy, the second phase will focus on the science and technology sector that will have more direct impact on the nation's economic development. Support will be provided for the development of high-calibre researchers (in particular, students in their Masters degree and Doctoral programmes), international exchange and cooperation, and innovative curriculum development.

Source: Kim and Rhee (2007)

BK21 has however come under strong criticism for favouring a small number of large-scale, research-orientated universities. One critic even argued that it is designed to support Seoul National University. Nevertheless, it is evident that BK21 has greatly improved the research capacity of universities. There is also some evidence that the amount of research funds that went into BK21 project teams had a positive impact on research productivity measured by research papers per faculty member. The number of research papers written by the faculty members involved in BK21 and published in Science Citation Index (SCI) journals increased from 3 765 in 1998 to 7 477 in 2003, comprising about 42% of the SCI journal articles of the nation (Kim & Rhee 2007: 128).

New initiative 2: New University for Regional Innovation (NURI)
NURI is a government-funded project for local universities that is aimed at diversification and specialisation, higher employment rates for local university graduates, and creating a greater role for local universities as centres of regional innovation, by strengthening ties within a region with local governments, companies and research institutions.

The government will invest US$1.2 million in the NURI project, and the fund will be allocated to 13 cities and provinces based on population and number of students and universities (Kim & Rhee 2007: 130). In 2004, 112 project groups were selected for their outstanding achievements. The Ministry of Education plans to conduct annual assessments and an interim assessment (in the third year of the project) which will include an assessment of budget execution and performance versus targets and make recommendations.

The impact of higher education on economic development

The South Korean experience of economic and parallel educational development is a classic example of the East Asian experience with catch-up industrial development. Mathews and Hu (2007) show that the mechanisms that were used to steer the development of industries and markets in this model involved states and state-sponsored institutions working closely with private-sector firms and markets.

Increasingly, the role of technological capacity development is coming to be viewed as central to the industrialising effort – and as the driving factor in East Asian success over the past half-century. In this setting, universities and public research institutes (PRIs) are two of the key institutions that shape economic development (Mathews & Hu 2007).

Universities played a very special role in East Asian development – not as drivers of innovation but as shapers of human capital formation. Throughout the past half-century, universities were at the forefront in training large numbers of highly-skilled graduates, who could be employed successfully by domestic firms seeking to enter global industries, by multinational corporations, and not least by the institutions steering the economy's industrial development. The foundation for this role played by the universities and newly established polytechnics was the steadily rising rate of adult literacy and numeracy, and the high quality of primary and secondary education. This is precisely what occurred in South Korea.

By contrast, the PRIs played the role of technology capture agencies and technology diffusion managers, going abroad to seek the technologies needed by local firms and building capabilities in those technologies which the PRIs passed across to the private sector as rapidly as possible. These institutes worked closely with domestic firms, developing their capacities to become technologically sophisticated players in their own right. PRIs drove the development of national innovative capacity in East Asian economies as they gradually moved from catching up and imitation to fast-follower innovation. For example, in South Korea in the 1970s, President Park recruited, at enormous cost, the finest South Korean scientists living abroad to establish the now foremost PRI in the country, the Korean Advanced Institute of Science and Technology (KAIST). In a short space of time, KAIST became the leading agency in the country for technology capture and transfer.

In the opening years of the 21st century, both universities and PRIs in East Asia in general, and in South Korea in particular, are undergoing further transformation as they are being encouraged to keep abreast of new technologies by patenting, publishing in scientific journals, and promoting spin-off enterprises.

Recalling the 'Latecomer Development Model' alluded to elsewhere (Pillay 2010), from 1950 to 2000 the East Asian economies fashioned a uniquely successful industrial development model in which the focus was clearly on science and technology as the primary productive forces. The idea was that these economies, as latecomers, could focus their industrial development on targeted catch-up efforts, industry by industry and technology by technology, drawing on the knowledge accumulated in the leading countries. The model was developed first in Japan, then rapidly adopted in South Korea and Taiwan (China), and later taken up by Singapore and to some extent elsewhere in Southeast Asia.

This model was a 20th century version of the catch-up strategies that had been perfected in the 19th century by European latecomer nations, particularly Germany, and the United States, as described by Gerschenkron (1962). The Gerschenkronian approach invites concentration on the issues that matter most, namely the building of new institutions and the pursuit of fresh strategies, depending on the situation when a country is attempting (or reattempting) its development push. Which institutions are most relevant in any given country or at any given time will vary. But the strategic use of institutions to overcome latecomer disadvantages can have a significant effect on development. With each successive entry by a latecomer country into the ranks of the industrial world, the barriers to entry change, and a different situation is bequeathed to those coming after. They must devise fresh strategies to get around the newly created barriers. Institutions and practices must then be discarded as soon as they have outlived their utility, so as to avoid the trap of allowing firms to become dependent on them.

Latecomer firms, like latecomer nations, exploit their late arrival to tap into advanced technologies, rather than replicating the entire preceding trajectory. They can accelerate their uptake and learning efforts through collaborative processes and the help of state agencies, thereby avoiding some of the organisational inertia that holds back their more established competitors. They thus develop strategy on the basis of the possibilities inherent in their latecomer status. The strategic goal of the latecomer is clear: catch up with the advanced firms and move as quickly as possible from imitation to innovation. This strategy has never been put into practice more effectively than by East Asian economies such as South Korea in their half-century of accelerated development.

As Mathews and Hu (2007) have described, the process of industrial development in East Asia can be viewed as one involving a series of choices, all conceived as strategic exercises in collective entrepreneurship. Entrepreneurship provides the appropriate framework for assessing development strategy, with an appropriate balance between the collective and individual facets of development. Latecomers seek to compensate for their shortcomings in technology and market sophistication through institutional innovation, under the guidance of development agencies, creating institutional solutions as problems are encountered. Examples include using export processing zones to promote foreign direct investment in manufacturing activities and using PRIs, such as KAIST in South Korea, to act as technology 'leveragers' and builders of national technological competences. Repeated applications of the processes of linking with commercial structures and leveraging knowledge from such sources teach latecomers to practice development as a process of collective entrepreneurship.

In keeping with the latecomer strategy, the East Asian economies never saw universities as agents of innovation, at least not during their half-century of accelerated catching up. Rather they saw universities as agents of human capital formation, viewing them as advanced training institutions and establishing them at a significant rate.

Although universities played the role of human capital formation institutions, the actual tasks associated with leveraging technology and diffusing it to the private sector were allocated to PRIs, which emerged as the central and defining institutions of the East Asian catch-up experience.

As documented in the expanding literature, universities and PRIs can be seen as contributing not only to their own innovation results but more fundamentally to the economy's innovative capacity; that is, capacity to sustain and enhance innovation as the industrial structure becomes more knowledge-based. Recent reforms in South Korean higher education are thus calculated to promote academic innovation through institutional and organisational reforms and therefore to drive the transition from manufacturing fast-follower to innovation-based technology developer.

In summary, the current reforms in South Korean higher education relating to quality, differentiation and relevance, and the attempts to stimulate research capacity in the universities, are designed to enhance South Korean human resource capacity to respond more creatively and fully to the challenges of innovation and the increasingly globalised and knowledge-based economy.

Drawing on the data and information presented in this chapter, some possbile implications for African countries, based on the South Korean experience, are outlined in the box below.

Box 8
The South Korean experience: Possible implications for Africa

1. **Linking economic and education planning:** The South Korean system clearly illustrates the benefits of maintaining a close link between economic and education planning. The government has been unashamedly interventionist in both sectors to promote overall social and economic development, with profound consequences over the past 40 years.

2. **Building higher education on a sound foundation of high-quality schooling:** The South Korean model shows how crucial high-quality schooling is for the development of a high-quality higher education system. While there are serious questions about overall quality in the South Korean higher education system, largely as a consequence of the rapid quantitative expansion, it has nevertheless been able to provide a large quantity of human capital to contribute to the country's rapid industrialisation efforts since the 1960s.

3. **South Korea's higher education system comprises a mix of private and public higher education institutions,** with the former dominating in terms of numbers. However, unlike many developing countries, the state-sponsored loan scheme supports students in both types of institutions.

4. **The role of higher education in economic development:** South Korean government higher education policy for most of the past four decades was to ensure that universities produced human capital for growth and development. The role of higher education institutions in research and innovation was minimal – the role of technology capture, transfer and development was left initially to the PRIs and then to private companies. This model is largely the one that prevails in Africa; that is, universities are largely the providers of human capital (graduates) with very little research and innovation taking place in higher education institutions. This raises the vexing question of why African countries have not been able to match the economic growth and development record of South Korea in the post-Second World War era.

5. **The role of networks in higher education in South Korea:** The hand of government is clearly visible in all components of the education system, including oversight of the private sector. Historically, an important network has been that between the relevant government ministries, the PRIs and the

South Korea

Box 8 (cont.)

large private sector companies (chaebol) with respect to R&D. Increasingly today, universities, and particularly the large public institutions, are becoming an important fourth component of this group as they develop their R&D capacity. Second, important linkages are developing directly between industry and universities, particularly through initiatives such as the Industry-Academia Collaboration. Finally, the third set of networks that is developing somewhat belatedly is that between universities, industry and regional governments in initiatives such as the Regional Innovation Committee and NURI. In summary, there has been a dramatic change in the nature of the higher education networks from one historically dominated by central government to one in which the private business sector and regional governments are starting to play an increasingly important role. Such initiatives are beginning to address both the role of universities in R&D and the challenge of regional equity in the quality of higher education institutions.

6. **Meeting the labour market needs of a knowledge-based economy:** It is evident that the higher education system has, to a great extent, not been able to produce the required quality of outputs for a knowledge-based economy. There is a large divergence between what employers are seeking of university graduates and their skills base. This is possibly the most important reason why South Korea has yet to make the leap to a growth pattern in which sectors demanding high-quality educated labour (the service sector generally through the information technology, finance and other sub-sectors) are dominating the composition of GDP. The lessons here are several. First, quality has inevitably been compromised by the rapid expansion of the system in a very short time. Second, expansion was accompanied by very little institutional differentiation. Third, it was expected that the private sector-dominated system would be better able to provide human resources in line with the needs of the economy, but this has clearly not happened. The ability of the government to 'steer' the system with appropriate incentives has not been possible in a system dominated by privately-financed institutions.

References

Aarrevaara T (2008) *Comments on First Draft of Finland Country Report* (P Pillay), Helsinki.

Aarrevaara T (2009) Note on *Differentiation actors in Finnish higher education*, Helsinki.

Ali-Yrko J & Hermans R (2002) *Nokia in the Finnish innovation system*. The Research Institute of the Finnish Economy, Discussion Paper No. 811, Helsinki.

Castells M and Himanen P (2001) The Finnish Model of the Information Society. *Sitra report Series* 17.

Clark JB (2008) Best values in public colleges. *Kiplinger's Personal Finance Magazine*. February 2008: 64–69. New York.

Davies J, Weko T, Kim L & Thulstrup E (2006) *Thematic Review of Tertiary Education: Finland Country Note*. Paris: Organization of Economic Co-operation and Development.

Dill, D (2008) *Comments on First Draft of North Carolina Report* (P Pillay), UNC-Chapel Hill.

Dobson, IR (2009) Finland: Radical changes for universities, *University World News*, www.universityworldnews.com, Issue 0081, 21 June.

Gerschenkron A (1962) *Economic Backwardness in Historical Perspective*. Cambridge, MA: Belknap Press.

Grubb WN, Sweet R, Gallagher M & Tuomi O (2006) Korea Country Note. *Thematic Review of Tertiary Education*. Paris: Organisation for Economic Co-operation and Development.

Interview: Ms Willa Dickens, Vice-President, Economic Workforce Development, North Carolina Community College System, March 2008.

Interview Notes, 2008. Finland; North Carolina; South Korea.

Jin M (2008) Comments on First Draft of Korea Country Report (P Pillay). *Korea Research Institute for Vocational Education and Training*, Seoul.

Jin M (2009) Note on *'The Differentiation of Higher Education in Korea'*, Seoul.

KEDI (Korea Education Development Institute) (2005) *Note on National University for Regional Development (NURI)*. Seoul: Korea Education Development Institute.

Kim A & Rhee B-S (2007) Meeting skill and human resource requirements. In Suh J and Chen DHC (eds) *Korea as a Knowledge Economy Evolutionary Process and Lessons Learned*. Seoul: Korea Development Instituo and World Bank Institute. pp 107 133.

Mathews JA & Hu M-C (2007) Universities and public research institutions as drivers of economic development in Asia. In Yusuf S and Nabeshima K (eds). *How Universities Promote Economic Growth*. Washington, DC: The World Bank.

MoE (Ministry of Education, Finland) (2005) *Thematic review of tertiary education: Country background report for Finland*. Report prepared for the OECD. Helsinki: Ministry of Education.

National Centre for Public Policy and Higher Education (2008) *Measuring Up*, San Jose, California, www.highereducation.org

NCSU (North Carolina State University) (2008) *North Carolina State University's extension, engagement, and economic development*. Office of Extension, Engagement and Economic Development, Raleigh.

Pillay P (2008) *Higher Education and Economic Development – A Review of the Literature*. Draft, unpublished. Cape Town: Centre for Higher Education Transformation.

Pillay P (2008a) *Report on North Carolina*, Draft, unpublished. Cape Town: Centre for Higher Education Transformation.

Pillay P (2008b) *Report on South Korea*, Draft, unpublished. Cape Town: Centre for Higher Education Transformation.

Pillay P (2010) *Higher Education and Economic Development: A Literature Review*. Cape Town: Centre for Higher Education Transformation.

Sadler, J (2009) Note on *'Constituent Institution Differentiation in the University of North Carolina'*, June. Chapel Hill, North Carolina.

Samsung Corporation (2007) *Samsung Annual Report 2007 – A Review of the Korean Economy in 2007*. Seoul.

Science and Technology Policy Council of Finland (2006) *Science, technology, innovation*. Helsinki.

Se-Jung O (2008) *High-level Human Resources Development Strategy of Korea*. Seoul National University.

STPC (Science and Technology Policy Council) of Finland (2006) *Science, Technology, Innovation*. Helsinki: Science and Technology Policy Council.

Suh J & Chen DHC (2007) *Korea as a Knowledge Economy – Evolutionary Process and Lessons Learned*. Korea Development Institute and World Bank Institute.

The World Bank (2008) *2008 Development Report*. Washington, D.C.

UNC (University of North Carolina) (2007) *UNC Tomorrow Commission: Final Report*. Chapel Hill: University of North Carolina.

United Nations Development Programme (2008) 2008 *Human Development Report*. New York.

Appendix 1: List of interviewees

Finland

The visit to Helsinki, Finland, was undertaken by Pundy Pillay (Centre for Higher Education Transformation, South Africa), James Nkata (Makerere University, Uganda) and Romulo Pinheiro (University of Oslo, Norway) in September 2008. The following individuals and institutions were visited:

- Professors Seppo Hölttä and Timo Aarrevaara, University of Tampere
- Dr Paulla Nybergh, Head of Innovation Division, Ministry of Employment and the Economy
- Dr Rita Asplund, Research Director, The Research Institute of the Finnish Economy
- Dr Antii Moisio, Principal Economist, Ms Tanja Kirjavainen and Dr Roope Uusitalo, Government Institute for Economic Research
- Mr Ossi Tuomi, Director of Development, University of Helsinki and former Secretary General, Finnish Higher Education Evaluation Council
- Dr Esko-Olavi Sepphala, Secretary General, Ministry of Education, Science and Technology Policy Council
- Professor Wim Naude, Senior Research Fellow, UNU-WIDER (World Institute for Development Economics Research)

South Korea

The visit to South Korea was undertaken by Nico Cloete (Director, CHET) and Pundy Pillay (CHET) in July 2008. The individuals and institutions visited are listed below:

Korean Council for University Education
- Dr Kang Byung-Woon, Director, Research Institute for Higher Education
- Dr Dong Kwang Kim, Director, Department of External Relations
- Ms Sarah Han, Researcher, Department of External Relations

Seoul National University
- Professor Se-Jung OH, Dean, College of Natural Sciences
- Professor Young Kuk, Vice-President, Research Affairs / Head, Industry-Academic Cooperation Foundation / CEO, SNU Industry Foundation

- Professor Keouk (Korbil) Kim, Department of Education and graduate students
- Professor Suk Ho Chung, Director, School of Mechanical Engineering and Aerospace Engineering

Samsung Economic Research Institute
- Dr Ji-Seong Ryu, Senior Research Fellow, Human Resources Management Department
- Ms Wuran Kang, Chief Researcher, HRM Department
- Dr Hyungmin Jung, Research Fellow, Macroeconomics

KDI-School
- Professor Ju Ho Lee, Education and Labour Market Economist

Korea Research Institute for Vocational Education and Training (KRIVET)
- Dr Mi-Sug Jin, Director, Department of Human Resources Research

Korea Education Development Institute (KEDI)
- Dr Jung Yoon Choi

North Carolina

The data for the North Carolina case study was collected by Pundy Pillay (CHET) during a prolonged visit to North Carolina during 2008. Two universities were visited: North Carolina State University and Duke University. The following individuals were interviewed:

- Dr Alan Mabe, Vice-President, Academic Planning and University-School Programmes, University of North Carolina System
- Ms Willa Dickens, Vice-President, Economic Workforce Development, North Carolina Community College System
- Dr James Zuiches, Vice-Chancellor, Office of Extension, Engagement and Economic Development, North Carolina State University
- Professor Helen Ladd, Professor of Social Policy, Terry Sanford Public Policy Institute, Duke University
- Professor Carol Kasworm, Head, Department of Adult and Higher Education, North Carolina State University
- Professor Charles Clotfelter, Professor of Public Policy, Terry Sanford Institute, Duke University

Appendix 2: Recommendations of the UNC Tomorrow Commission

Global readiness

With regard to global readiness, the recommendations and suggested strategies were the following:

Recommendation 1

UNC should prepare its students for successful professional and personal lives in the 21st century, equipping them with the tools they will need to adapt to the ever-changing world.

Suggested strategies:

- Improve student proficiency in 'soft skills', including oral and written communication, critical thinking and analytical reasoning, problem-solving, creativity and innovation, teamwork and collaboration, work ethic and professionalism, financial literacy, information literacy, and digital literacy.
- Improve student proficiency in 21st-century knowledge, emphasising science, technology, engineering and mathematics.
- Create a state-wide task force that partners with business, non-profit organisations and faculty to develop a strategic plan for integrating 'soft skills' throughout the curriculum, from general education through majors and graduate programmes by:
  - Identifying existing successful UNC centres and programmes to serve as models of areas of soft-skills development throughout UNC.
  - Creating a state-wide council of staff and writing directors from across UNC to identify successful strategies for writing and literacy programmes, and to work with appropriate staff to improve campus programmes and enhance students' writing and literacy competencies.
  - Developing ways that business can strengthen its role in providing resources (people and money) to assist universities in preparing students to enter the workforce.
  - Recognising and rewarding the role of the humanities and arts education in developing 'soft skills' by strengthening the commitment of resources to the liberal arts.
  - Increasing emphasis on entrepreneurial thinking and learning skills for students to equip them to adapt to the rapidly changing economy.
  - Providing appropriate faculty development opportunities and support to

encourage faculty to use pedagogical methods that have been proven to be more effective with the changing student population (active learning, collaborative teams, problem-based learning, client-based projects, etc.).
- Incorporating experiential learning opportunities across degree programmes and throughout curricula through such activities as internships, job-shadowing, undergraduate research, community and service projects, project-based and active learning, work-study programmes, studying abroad, and business mentors.
- Promoting and rewarding civic engagement, leadership and community service among students, faculty and staff.
- Developing tools that assess and verify students' understanding, application and mastery of 21st-century life skills needed in every professional endeavour.
- Maximising resources of career centres on campuses and integrating career counselling with academic advising.

Recommendation 2
UNC programmes, especially research programmes, should be globally competitive to ensure that they are globally relevant and significant.

Suggested strategies:

- Maintain and strengthen the quality and high standards of academic curricula, research, and scholarship activities to world standards of excellence.
- Continue to expand basic and applied research activities consistent with the priorities and missions of UNC campuses.
- Encourage faculty, when appropriate, to make their research available to the public at large on a local, national and global basis in a language that the public can understand and use.

Access to higher education
Recommendation 1
UNC should increase its access to its educational programmes – including academic courses, degree programmes at all levels and certificate programmes – for traditional students, non-traditional students and lifelong learners.

Suggested strategies:

- Broaden and innovate delivery of courses and degree programmes through additional online and distance education programmes (including expanding online courses and degree programmes offered through UNC online), evening and weekend classes and programmes, improved facility utilisation, and other flexible options such as courses of varying length (e.g. intensive six-week courses) that meet the needs of working adults and targeted groups such as full-time employers, corporations and government agencies.
- Explore the feasibility of establishing satellite campuses and higher education centres, especially in high-need, underserved areas.

- Recognise that the lack of access to full broadband internet service in some regions of the state limits access to online and distance education programmes at the school, community college and university levels; and utilise existing resources in increasing broadband access.
- Secure funding for year-round enrolment to maximise use of existing facilities and accelerate students toward degree completion.
- Promote the development of collaborative partnerships with corporations, and other entities in which appropriate degree and continuing education programmes are developed and offered to these identified pools of learners.
- Develop more partnerships with private colleges and universities (e.g. joint degree programmes).
- Encourage increased utilisation of UNC's historically black campuses by all of the state's population, including strategies for increased recruitment of high-achieving public school students for enrolment in historically black universities.
- Research and develop evidence-based strategies to engage individuals who are not pursuing higher education to re-enter the education system.

Recommendation 2
UNC should continue ongoing efforts with the NCCCS to strengthen and streamline articulation between the two systems so as to develop a more seamless relationship.

Suggested strategies:

- Strengthen and broaden the comprehensive articulation agreement to ensure more seamless transition for students transferring between community colleges and UNC institutions.
- Improve academic advising for community college students to better prepare them for transfer to a four-year degree programme/institution.
- Explore the use of electronic advising on course and degree requirements across the community college and UNC systems.
- Increase the number of 2+2 programmes and other joint programmes between the UNC and community colleges.
- Support the NCCCS's efforts to increase associate degree offerings.
- Support increased funding for community college classes in core and high-need curricula.
- Explore the use of joint and shared facilities on both community college and UNC campuses.

Recommendation 3
UNC should increase the educational attainment of all under-represented populations, especially African-American male and Hispanic students.

Suggested strategies:

- Investigate where UNC is losing representation in its student enrolment compared to the general population, such as among male students, and identify specific strategies for increasing the educational attainment of those under-represented populations.
- Develop strategies to address the unique problems confronting the state's African-American male population, including:
  - Leveraging UNC expertise to identify specific intervention strategies, including recruitment and retention strategies.
  - Inventorying existing efforts within the UNC system and assessing their effectiveness.
  - Exploring best practices nationally.
  - Working with the state's public school system to improve educational outcomes for African-American males.
  - Devising strategies to increase the minority presence in higher education, particularly African-American males.
  - Increasing the number of African-American faculty at all UNC institutions and helping increase the number of African-American public school teachers.
  - Identifying, within the UNC system, existing successful outreach and student recruitment efforts within the African-American community.
- Identify specific strategies for serving Hispanic students and increasing their educational attainment.

Recommendation 4
UNC should help ensure that all students are better prepared to enter and succeed academically in college.

Suggested strategies:

- Maintain and increase the quality of a UNC education.
- Raise admission standards, expand conditional admission programmes, work with the NCCCS to accept more students not yet ready to enter a university, and hold all UNC institutions to high academic standards.
- Provide better information about college admission requirements and offer stronger academic advising at middle- and high-school level.
- Develop a clearer public understanding of 'college readiness' in its many forms so that expectations for college attainment are better understood.
- Upgrade and expand college-readiness programmes such as summer bridge programmes, early college programmes, online 'Learn and Earn', and early college programmes for high school students.
- Implement, monitor and assess ongoing initiatives to improve graduation and retention rates.
- Strengthen programmes that provide additional academic support to students in need of special assistance.

- Collaborate with the North Carolina State Board of Education and North Carolina Department of Public Instruction on improvements to the state's public school system.
- Improve student advising at the public school, community college and university levels to build better awareness about career options, workforce demands and 'soft skills' needed for success in the 21st-century economy.
- Reduce barriers to seamless transition between community colleges and UNC institutions.

Improving public education
Recommendations
- UNC should improve the quantity, quality and geographic distribution of public school teachers.
- UNC should help address the shortage of science and mathematics teachers, especially in rural areas.
- UNC should strengthen efforts, in cooperation with the North Carolina State Board of Community Colleges and the NCCCS, the North Carolina State Board of Education, and the North Carolina Department of Public Instruction, to enhance the teaching skills of public faculty and the leadership skills of public school administrators.
- UNC should leverage its expertise and increase collaborations with the State Board of Education and Department of Public Instruction to lower the state's dropout rate and improve academic achievement in all North Carolina public schools, especially those that are high-priority and low-performing.
- UNC should strengthen partnerships with the State Board of Education, the North Carolina Department of Public Instruction, the NCCCS, and the state's independent colleges and universities to develop a seamless educational continuum from pre-school through to higher education.

Economic transformation
Recommendation 1
UNC should increase its capacity and commitment to respond to and lead economic transformation and community development.

Suggested strategies:

- Promote and educate communities and students (both at the public school and at the higher education levels) in entrepreneurship and innovation to ensure that they can adjust to and compete in the knowledge-based global economy.
- Link faculty expertise to regional economic strategies.
- Facilitate access to UNC expertise in economic and community development initiatives.
- Develop communications mechanisms to facilitate better interaction between UNC and business, industry, community, government and non-profit sectors.
- Encourage the faculty to make its research available to the public in an accessible and understandable form – on a local, national and global basis.

- Encourage, reward and provide support for faculty research and practice at all UNC institutions in applied public policy analysis focusing on important regional and state-wide issues, including that done in partnership with or on behalf of non-profit and public sector organisations.
- Work closely with government and non-profit organisations in addressing community challenges.
- Enhance and streamline dissemination and commercialisation of UNC technologies and discoveries to fuel development of new and emerging industries and job creation.

Recommendation 2
UNC should focus specific effort on meeting the needs of rural and under served areas of the state.

Suggested strategies:

- Increase adult-learning opportunities, educational programmes and degree delivery to residents of rural areas.
- Develop specific plans to assist in locating high-need graduates (e.g. teachers and healthcare professionals) in under-served areas.
- Work collaboratively with state organs to improve public school student performance in low-performing schools and school districts.
- Target UNC institution degree programmes and faculty research in rural North Carolina to stimulate growth of new and emerging industries and enhance existing industries.
- Leverage faculty expertise across UNC to help address pressing needs of rural areas, such as health disparities and poverty rates.

Recommendation 3
UNC should seek to align appropriate campus programmes with the strategic economic plans (including sector and cluster plans) of their regions and the state, recognising the unique differences and challenges of the state's economic and geographic regions.

Suggested strategies:

- Develop an internet-based portal that industries can use to find specific expertise at all UNC campuses.
- Identify an appropriate individual at each campus charged with overseeing that campus' economic transformation activities; and require each campus to report annually on its efforts to enhance the economic transformation of the state.
- Develop degree programmes and continuing education programmes to meet the regional and state-wide needs of specific employers and business sectors.
- Institutionalise communication mechanisms between UNC and regional business and industry sectors.

- Build on the successful model of UNC's collaboration with North Carolina's biotech industry in developing additional collaborations with business and industry sectors (both existing and emerging) to target UNC degree and continuing education programmes and research activities, where appropriate, to enhance and stimulate economic growth.
- Leverage UNC expertise and resources in enhancing regional and state-wide economic transformation strategies (such as in regional economic development planning) and stimulating regional economic opportunities (such as research efforts and education programmes targeted at new and emerging industries and entrepreneurship).
- Support increased collaborations between the private sector and UNC's historically black universities.

Health

Recommendation 1
UNC should lead in improving health and wellness in North Carolina.

Suggested strategies:

- Apply to the university's healthcare systems the best available practices to promote a healthier population in health communities through prevention and direct care.
- Prioritise programmes and interventions in UNC's healthcare systems and throughout its leadership in UNC's medical schools, the schools of public health, social work, nursing, pharmacy and dentistry to help improve the health of all North Carolinians.
- Use proven programmes and mechanisms to improve access to healthcare, and help educate the public about model systems that enhance access.
- Make UNC institutions models of health and wellness through food service, recreation and wellness programmes for students, faculty and staff.
- Focus research efforts on health disparities among population groups and among geographic regions in the state.

Recommendation 2
UNC should educate more health professionals.

Recommendation 3
UNC should lead in utilising health information to improve health and wellness in North Carolina.

Environment

Recommendation 1
UNC should embrace environmental sustainability as a core value among its institutions.

Recommendation 2
UNC should leverage its existing research expertise to address critical environmental and energy issues.

Recommendation 3
UNC should increase community awareness of environmental and sustainability issues.

www.ingramcontent.com/pod-product-compliance
Lightning Source LLC
Chambersburg PA
CBHW080252030426

42334CB00023BA/2795